Search for Identity

Earl Jabay

Search for Identity

SEARCH FOR IDENTITY

© 1981 by Earl Jabay

Library of Congress Catalog Card Number 81-83581
ISBN 0-88021-038-9

Ronald N. Haynes Publishers, Inc.
Palm Springs, California 92263

Originally published by:
Zondervan Publishing House
Grand Rapids, Michigan

Printed in the United States of America

Acknowledgment is gratefully made to the following for permission to use the following copyrighted material:

BEACON PRESS, for quotations from Viktor Frankl, *Man's Search for Meaning: An Introduction to Logotherapy,* © 1959, 1962 by Viktor Frankl.

THE MACMILLAN CO., for quotations from Edward A. Strecker and Kenneth E. Appel, *Discovering Ourselves,* © 1962.

HARPER & Row, for quotations from Meister Eckhart, translated by Raymond Blakney, © 1941; and Paul Scherer, *Love Is a Spendthrift,* © 1961.

GRUNE AND STRATTON, and STELLA CHESS, for a quotation from Stella Chess, *An Introduction to Child Psychiatry,* © 1959.

The Division of Christian Education of the National Council of the Churches of Christ, for Scripture quotations from The Revised Standard Version, © 1946 and 1952.

Foreword

We are pleased to introduce and to commend the Rev. Earl Jabay and his book to you who have met his writing before in *The Church Herald*, and who will be glad to see it here again, with considerable additions in a more permanent form; and also to you who meet him here for the first time.

The author writes with a compassionate concern out of his own personal experiences with all sorts and conditions of people. His love for people and his understanding of their needs has developed in him a strong desire to help them face up to their real (not imaginary) needs and problems, and then to lead them to fulfillment of life. Guided by Christian convictions based upon a Biblical interpretation of life, he combines here a pastor's experiences, a chaplain's findings and a scholar's understanding of psychology, to provide us with directions in "a search for identity." He knows something not alone of the native emptiness of the human heart, but of the God who comes to fill that vacuum with His grace and truth. He has come to some of his conclusions through agony of soul, hammered out on the anvil of stern reality. Running like a thread through all these conversations with his readers is the theme of Augustine's prayer: "Lord,

Thou hast made us for Thyself, and our hearts are restless until they rest in Thee."

This book, while it draws on the experiences and conclusions of one who has dealt with persons having peculiar and abnormal personality problems, is intended to help all of us take a more objective look at ourselves, to ask ourselves questions we usually dismiss or ignore, really to understand ourselves, and then to act upon that understanding. We see something of ourselves in the brief case references and incidents in other lives, through which the author intends to lead us to find for ourselves a more "authentic Christian living." A deeper understanding of ourselves, and of our common human nature, will also make it possible for us to assist others all about us who face the conflicts of a cultured but cruel world.

LOUIS H. BENES
Editor, *The Church Herald*

Preface

This book contains some of the lessons learned through the day-to-day experiences in the mental hospital at which I am a chaplain. Rich treasures of wisdom and knowledge have been given to us through the lives of people with emotional illness, through the body of psychiatric knowledge, and above all, through the resources of the Christian Faith and the Holy Scriptures. I invite you to join me as we sit at the feet of this Faculty and learn their secrets.

Our Faculty, as I will attempt to show, knows something about the search for one's identity. No small part of the problem of those who receive treatment for emotional problems is that they have lost their sense of identity. As one man put it, "I am looking for a feeling of somebodyness." When he said this I recalled the words of Peter: "You were no people but now you are God's people; once you had not received mercy but now you have received mercy" (I Peter 2:10). We all were nobodies until God, through Christ, made us somebodies. That is what we want to talk about in this book.

All but a few of these chapters have already been published in the weekly publication of the Reformed Church in America, the *Church Herald.* Permission has been granted to republish these essays in book form by the editor, Dr. Louis Benes, who advised and helped me in so many ways. Mention must also be made of the stimulation and instruction given me by my colleagues at the New Jersey Neuro-Psyciatric Institute.

EARL JABAY
Princeton, N.J.

Contents

Part I
Who You Are

Chapter One
"Who Am I?"

THE FIRST TIME I visited a mental hospital, the chaplain took me through the wards and explained the illnesses of some of the people. I have forgotten most of what the chaplain said because my anxieties were considerably aroused, but one statement made a deep impression on me and I will never forget it.

"The basic question which these people are asking," he said, "is 'Who am I?'" He went on to explain that one man thought he was Christ; another thought he was Napoleon; another thought he was an animal. These notions, of course, were pure fantasy but they were and perhaps still are believed by these patients. The mass of people reject these answers and rightly contend that Christ appeared 2,000 years ago, that Napoleon is dead and that this human being who stood with us in the ward was not an animal.

But who then is he? Suppose he would say, "I am Adam Mudd." Giving his name helps a little to distinguish him from other people, but this does not really answer the question "Who are you?" unless you want to argue that a person is his name. But that, I submit, is nonsense. I am not my name. I *have* a name but *am not* my name. If you misspell my name you do not damage me. It's just a name. When a woman marries she changes her name but not her person.

Suppose that our friend would tell us the truth about himself and say, "I am schizophrenic." Not even this would do, because a person is not the same as his problem. Problems change with the years but a person is still himself. To identify him with his problem is quite as foolish as to identify him with his name. Human beings are people, not problems.

Nor are we people our occupations. If our friend says, "I am a policeman," and has the papers and a badge to prove it, all this means is that we now know what he does. But again, we are not what we do. We are responsible for what we do, but we are not the deed itself because we are people – persons who act but are not the acts themselves.

To some this may seem as though we are speaking nonsense or at best dwelling on useless fine points. We are dealing, however, with a most basic idea – the separation of the person from his world. Most of our problems come from the fact that in our minds we merge the two – the person and his world. God created us to be human spirits who, on the one hand, would commune with Him who is Holy Spirit, and, on the other hand, would "subdue the earth." Too often we allow ourselves to be subdued by our world and the things in it (our feelings, problems, occupations, etc.). Our fall from a position *under* God and *over* the world causes us to identify ourselves with our world rather than God. The inevitable result of "misplacing" ourselves in God's world is that we lose the sense of identity which our Maker intended us to have. We identify with our world to such a degree that we become swallowed up by it.

God made us human spirits. That is our identity. Our origin is another world. Our parent is not the earth. God is our parent. "The Lord God formed man...and breathed into his nostrils the breath of life; and man became a living being" (Genesis 2:7). The words *living being* are a translation of the Hebrew word *ruach* which means spirit, wind, air. We are spirits made in the "image of God." As God is Spirit, man is also spirit—human spirit. Job says: "It is the spirit in a man, the breath of the Almighty, that makes him understand" (Job 32:8). One could go on to quote texts in both Testaments to establish the biblical witness to man as a divinely created human spirit. But in the end we would have to face the fact that this affirmation can be made only by a religious believing person. A request for proof is as absurd as the request to prove that God exists. Both God and man are undemonstrable because both are spirits.

To say that man is human spirit is as close as we can get to an answer to our question "Who am I?" If we really work with this knowledge and go on to understand that each human spirit may make real, valid choices with regard to his world from which he is separate, then we will be helped in the living of these lives to God's glory. So let us now consider the human spirit in action as a "choosing creature," to use Karl Jaspers' definition of man.

Chapter Two
Choosing Your Attitude

ONE SUNDAY as I came out of church, a woman called me aside and said: "Pastor, I'm terribly distressed. I don't see any sense in what I am doing. Look at me. I've been a patient in this mental hospital for 20 years! I'm nothing. You—you have a nice position as chaplain. You got it good. But me? I'm a total waste."

Her problem? Meaninglessness.

We all struggle against it.

How would you have responded to my parishioner?

Understand that she is a Christian. She knows her Bible a bit too. I have no doubts about her commitment to Christ and her love for His church. She is aware of and thankful for the fact that God loves her, accepts her and understands her problem. Moreover, I discovered that she has prayed much about this problem of meaninglessness but she is still without a solution to it.

Let me tell you how I responded to her and you can compare it with your own approach.

"No wonder you do not see meaning in your life!" I

began. "You have set your life up wrongly." Then I waited.

"What do you mean?" she asked, picking up interest in what I was saying.

"I mean, you've missed the point of being a Christian."

"I don't understand. In which way?"

She was now ready for some help. Rarely can we help people until they are ready to receive help.

I decided to come quickly to the point with her. "As a Christian, you feel you ought to be blessed with certain things—perhaps a home or marriage or a successful occupation. If you had one or all of these, you feel you would find meaning in life."

"Sure I would," she commented, "and wouldn't you too?"

"Of course I like success, but it is possible that someday I would be a patient here with you. Then what? All my symbols of success would be taken from me. But this does not mean my life has no more meaning. Neither am I finished as a person."

My parishioner felt I was not really helping her because I was too negative. I agreed.

"Meaning in life," I continued, "is achieved not by reaching certain occupational goals but by choosing Christian attitudes toward one's world." I went on to explain that one's world is his environment and situation. My parishioner's world is living as a chronic patient in a hospital with both the limitations and opportunities of that environment. She is not free to go and come as so many of us are privileged to do. Yet she has, as we all do in "impossible" situations, a *freedom to choose her attitude toward her world*. She can choose to be resentful, courageous, angry, contented, fearful, helpful, unsociable—any attitude at all.

"If I understand you, Pastor, you are saying that I am free to choose any attitude I wish to select toward this hospital. Hmmm. I'll have to think about that one awhile...but it may be worth it!" I encouraged her to continue her search for meaning, for one can find meaning in any situation, no matter how disastrous.

Let me ask you—do you think you could have found meaning in life during World War II if you had been a prisoner awaiting the gas chambers of Buchenwald? A famous doctor of the soul, Dr. Viktor Frankl, was in just such a "world," and this is what he writes:

> We who lived in concentration camps can remember the men who walked through the huts comforting others, giving away their last piece of bread. They may have been few in number, but they offer sufficient proof that everything can be taken from a man but one thing: the last of the human freedoms—to choose one's attitude in any given set of circumstances, to choose one's own way.[1]

It is not enough, however, merely to choose one's own way. The trick in life is to choose sets of attitudes which our Lord Jesus Christ has both recommended and empowered us to receive through the Holy Spirit. Such attitudes, though they will not always supply us with what we want (such as a discharge from a mental hospital) will invariably cause us to be "more than conquerors through him who loved us." This is why *nothing* "will be able to separate us from the love of God in Christ Jesus our Lord" (Romans 8:37,39).

[1] *Man's Search for Meaning—An Introduction to Logotherapy,* copyright 1959, 1962 by Viktor Frankl (Boston: Beacon Press, 1962), p. 62.

Jesus encouraged us in so many ways to choose these victorious attitudes. He talked, for example, about a widow who was constantly being rebuffed by a judge who refused to vindicate her. The widow chose her attitudes: courage, persistence, continual pleas, hope. She used her last freedom. The parable ends with the searching words: "Nevertheless, when the Son of man comes, will he find faith on the earth?" (Luke 18:1-8). In other words, will the right attitudes have been selected?

All of us who are weary and heavy laden with the crushing weight of unworkable attitudes toward our worlds, may bring them again to the Saviour and learn of Him the attitudes which bring meaning, brightness, hope and rest for our souls. Whether we go and learn of Him or flee from His presence, we are making a choice. To be a human being inevitably involves making choices. It is a part of our identity. God created us as choosing, selecting, deciding creatures.

We now turn to inquire about the freedom of such choices.

Chapter Three
Freedom of Choice

THE WORDS *freedom of choice* refer to a condition in which we are not coerced in our decision making. Coerced decisions are ones in which something outside of our conscious control constrains us to decide in a way in which we ourselves would not choose. There is an important distinction between a decision reached under coercion and one reached under influence. Coercion damages the exercise of the will. Influence leaves the will free but informed of factors it should know.

The point of this chapter is that man possesses an uncoerced freedom of choice but one influenced by his world and yet foreordained by God.

Such a position is not popular today because of the strong influence of Freudianism. Sigmund Freud believed that our choices are foreordained by hidden psychic forces. He asserts that "there is nothing undetermined in the psychic life." This means that whatever we feel, say or do as people is the product of the instinctual forces in the unconscious mind. Freud saw the sexual instincts as the basic life-promoting drive in us, and for this reason, he ascribed the source of most of our behavior to the sexual drive.

If the instincts in man determine his choices and behavior, then we as persons have no real freedom. And since the loss of freedom implies the loss of responsibility, we are no longer responsible creatures. On this basis we can evade responsibility for our choices, because they are foreordained by our instinctual feelings. One must then speak of his behavior as perhaps unhealthy but never as sinful, for the latter implies a choice of evil for which one must be held responsible, and good Freudians never say that. But we are thankful to find some inconsistent Freudians who do talk about evil and responsibility.

Mr. Z is an illustration of this point concerning freedom of choice. He came to his pastor with a "girl problem." He wanted very much to find a woman and marry her but something always got in the way and here he was, pushing 40 and still unmarried. "The reason for this," said Mr. Z, "has something to do with my early life as a child. I had a terrible childhood." And with this statement, he launched into a long tale about his delinquent parents. They were "sick," he claimed. "They messed me up." He felt himself victimized and, even worse, locked in this problem because of what they had done to him.

It took a long time before Mr. Z came to see that the problem was not his parents but himself – that whatever problems he had today were largely the results of choices he had made. True, his parents were not always the best influence upon him, but no parent would ever have been able to satisfy the insatiable demands of Mr. Z as a child. The truth of the matter was that *he* was messed up, not his parents. Light and hope began to break through when he began to see that since he had chosen his way into the problem, he could choose his way out, instincts notwithstanding.

Should our choices perhaps be foreordained by a wiser person than ourselves? There is a school of "human engineering" which takes this position. Psychologists have done a great deal of study on conditioned reflexes, "brainwashing" and the actual control of human behavior. Already in 1949 scientists were speaking of the "approaching ability to control men's thoughts with precision." When Sir Winston Churchill read this he commented, "I shall be very content to be dead before that happens." A wise man, Churchill!

The movement toward having an elite caste of scientists controlling masses of robot-like people is on the way. B.F. Skinner, Professor of Psychology at Harvard University has written *Walten Two* to show how a community of 600 people could be psychologically conditioned to live the good life. George Orwell's *1984* is the tragic tale of what could happen to society if we delegate our God-given freedom to choose to other people. We would become mere automata—empty, dehumanized, depersonalized people doing the will of some self-appointed Big Brother.

In order to withstand these forces in our culture, we desperately need people who are aware of their instinctual strivings as well as sensitive to good social influences upon them, but who will, nonetheless, make their own decisions under God. It happens more often than we think that people will allow themselves to become enslaved to their feelings or to other people. One's environment must be taken into account but ideally we should act upon it rather than assume a passive posture in what we like to think is a deterministic world.

Are our choices and our destinies foreordained by God? We may be thankful that they are! The Lord spare us all from the coercive determinism of our instincts and other people. Far better that we are in the hands of the Lord!

God has revealed to us an infinitely wise arrangement in the doctrine of foreordination.

On the one hand, we have freedom of choice. "Behold, I stand at the door and knock..." The choices we make are significant, real, and we bear full responsibility for them. On the other hand, God chooses us and lovingly ordains what comes to pass in our lives according to His sovereign will. "He chose us in him before the foundation of the world." "Even the hairs of your head are all numbered."[1]

Each concept is true; each is valid. It is when we try to blend them that we run into much difficulty. But the difficulty is more in our minds than in our lives.

In practice, each human spirit freely makes choices and bears responsibility for them. And God carries out His sovereign plan for us all — yet never coercively because God respects the freedom He has given us. Just *how* God guides us in life is a mystery, but the Christian is not interested in logical answers so much as the actual operation of providential grace in his life.

[1] Revelation 3:20; Ephesians 1:4; Matthew 10:30; Luke 12:7.

This knowledge – that God has acted and still acts today in human destiny – along with the fact that we are called upon to make significant choices in that destiny, means security and challenge in a Christian's life. Decisions and choices on our part are worked out in the dialogue of our spirits with the Holy Spirit. That dialogue takes place within us. We become aware of it in the introspective life, to which we now turn our thoughts.

Chapter Four
Introspection

In a time now past, the Japanese tea houses were used for Buddhist worship. As the devout worshiper would crawl into the small tea house, he would immediately be confronted with a sign saying *Kan Kok Ka*. "Look to where you are standing." It is roughly equivalent to the words of Thales, *gnothi sauton*, "Know thyself." Today we would put it, "Be introspective!" Frankly, I like the Buddhist and Grecian expressions best, but for the purposes of this chapter, the word *introspection* will be used. It simply means "looking within."

What can we learn from healthy introspection? I am talking now about an individual person who is in a suitable situation to engage in some honest reflection upon himself. As he contemplates himself, what does he find?

He becomes aware, first, that he is an introspector. Let us not quickly hasten past this first discovery because it is truly a great find. It is the discovery of his spirit—what he essentially is. It is he as a human spirit who contemplates whatever thoughts and feelings are in his mind. What we are doing here is drawing a line of separation between the human spirit who does the introspecting and the things introspected. That which is introspected cannot do the introspecting; this action is performed by one's spirit which can stand apart from one's thoughts and feelings. As the Book of Proverbs says: "The spirit of man is the lamp of the Lord, searching all his innermost parts" (20:27). The human spirit can do this because, like the divine Spirit in whose image he is made, spirits are not limited by such things as space, matter and time.

We also learn something else as we become introspective. We find a countless array of thoughts and feelings. Theoretically, all that we have ever learned or felt is now open to us. We might again see ourselves as little children playing on the kitchen floor, experiencing again the secure (or insecure) feeling we felt at that time. We might remember a dragon in a dream we once had. If a psychologist were to hypnotize us, we could be taken back to the experience even of intrauterine life in our mothers. And, of course, all that has happened in later years is stored away, if not in the conscious, then in the unconscious mind. We are talking about the millions, perhaps billions of sensations which have come to us in our lifetime – all this is theoretically available to us as we introspect.

The important thing to observe is that you and I as human spirits are *not* these thoughts and feelings. We *are* human spirits who *have* feelings, but we *are not* these feelings.

Would you believe that most people do not believe this? It is true. I recall the case of a man who would look at his wife and have a terrible thought about her. He felt the impulse to take a knife and stab her! He realized that this was murder and suffered under a heavy load of guilt, so much so that he was becoming a nervous wreck. Finally, he went to his pastor and confessed, "I am a murderer!"

"Whom did you murder?" asked the pastor.

"No one yet," he said, "but I keep thinking about murdering my wife and I have a strong impulse to do it — so I must be a murderer at heart!"

And then the pastor made a very wise response: "No, not a murderer at heart, just a murderer in fantasy. You are a dream-murderer, a make-believe murderer."

This husband had made the fatal mistake of assuming that *he was his feelings*. You recall how he said it: "I am a murderer." This was not true. He should have said: "I am a person who has murderous feelings toward my wife but I have not yet acted upon my feelings."

Am I now condoning these murderous thoughts or perhaps flippantly passing over their sinful character? I do not mean to do so. I am aware of our Lord's teaching "that every one who looks at a woman lustfully has already committed adultery with her in his heart" (Matthew 5:28). The same would apply to murder. My interest, however, is in making clear distinctions between the person, the feelings of that person, and the deeds done by that person. They are all different. When one becomes confused about them and lumps them all together as did the husband in our example, a needless and crushing weight of guilt tortures the person. It was the merciful desire of this man's pastor to lighten the guilt by drawing the proper distinctions.

So let us imagine that this husband now understands that he is a person and did not actually murder his wife. That leaves him with a murderous thought-feeling (the words are hyphenated because every thought is charged with some feeling). What might we now say to this man? How might we help and thereby love him?

If I were his pastor, I would listen sympathetically while both he and I got acquainted with his thought-feelings. Hopefully, my calm acceptance of them would lessen his fears somewhat. Now since he understands that he is a human spirit, I would point out that by linking his spirit to the divine Spirit through faith and prayer, God and he can transcend the power of his thought-feelings. We would pray for God's power unto the healing of this man and petition the Almighty to save him from the guilt and power of his sins.

But there is more to do. You recall that the thought-feeling of this man was recurrent. "I keep thinking about murdering my wife." This may mean that there is an illness on the emotional level of this man. These thought-feelings may be obsessive—a condition in which a person is continually haunted by the same thought in what is felt to be an irresistible manner. Such a struggle is, frankly, more than we can hope to handle. It is a problem beyond our solution. Our appeal must immediately be not to self but to God who is all-powerful. We must surrender both ourselves and the problem to God.

Thus, with a full use of the means available — counsel, surrender, prayer and faith, we would trust that God would bring such healing to this man that he would gain both an awareness and a control of his thought-feelings unto a more productive and God-glorifying life. This is the goal of introspection.

Chapter Five
Introspection (continued)

ABOUT 100 YEARS AGO, Sigmund Freud opened his medical office for the practice of psychiatry. Though his ideas quickly spread over Europe, America has always been the most fertile soil, not only for Freudian psychiatry but for psychology in general. Looking back, it seems that America was just waiting to be counseled. People, large numbers of whom were in real pain, were looking eagerly for help with their emotional problems. They were in the mood for introspection.

What began as a small stream with Freud has become a flood of people-helpers. Today in America, we have an army of 55,000 psychiatrists and psychologists offering professional help to around 34 million people who are problems to themselves and others. The professionals have organized themselves into approximately 250 different schools, few of which have anything good to say about each other. The only technique which is common to all is the suggestion to look within – to seek the truth about one's self through introspection.

No doubt there are many reasons why people are reaching out for psychological help, but here I wish to mention just one. People as never before are searching for their true identity. They are asking the question, Who am I? They want to find their true selves. Self-knowledge is their paramount and in some ways laudable goal in life. Modern psychiatry and psychology, however, failed miserably in helping people answer these questions. The professionals have not delivered on their promise to help. "Vain is the help of man. (Ps. 60:11)."

The advice of Scripture is quite at variance with modern mental technicians. Surprisingly, there is very little Scripture which urges us to look within. The biblical thrust seems to be twofold: (1) that *God* rather than man is the searcher of human hearts;[1] (2) that though we are to look within, it is more important to look *up* to God in faith.[2]

There are passages such as "Thou desirest truth in the inward being" (Psalm 51:6), and "Examine yourselves, to see whether you are holding to your faith" (II Corinthians 13:5), but these passages enjoin a test of one's life in the presence of God rather than the mere acquisition of self-knowledge as an end in itself. One looks in vain for passages similar to the Zen-Buddhist "Look to where you are standing" or the Grecian "Know thyself." These statements prove that the way of introspection was known to the ancients, but strangely, the Lord did not reveal this as the main

[1] Chronicles 28:9; Pslams 26:2; 139:1,23; Jeremiah 17:10; I Corinthians 2:10.
[2] Proverbs 3:5; Hebrews 12:2.

path for His people to tread. The people of God through the ages have found their identity and true character primarily through confrontation with and faith in God, and only secondarily through introspection.

This is not to disparage honest introspection which is valid and helpful to a point, both for those who bear the name of Christ and those who do not know Him. But unless introspection is coupled with a personal confrontation with Deity, true self-knowledge cannot be gained. John Calvin had a deep understanding of this in the first pages of his *Institutes* where he asserts that "it is plain that no man can arrive at the true knowledge of himself, without having first contemplated the divine character, and then descended to the consideration of his own." When Calvin speaks, as he does here, of the contemplation of the divine character, he means a deeply religious experience in which the sinner meets a forgiving God through the mercies of Jesus Christ.

Such an encounter with God spells the end of the search for our identity, for the encounter reveals it to us. We know ourselves to be in God's family. We are people restored to His image, spirits who feel known by the Father of spirits and who in turn know Him.

Suddenly we understand that the road to a knowledge of our identity is not a direct one. If we seek to know ourselves by direct introspection, we become lost in a maze created by the countless thoughts and feelings of our cluttered minds. The discovery of our identity is not something which we can earn if only our introspection is thorough enough. Knowledge of our identity is more like a gift. The gift comes when it is not sought; it comes indirectly.

One must first stand in the presence of God and there know Him, deal with Him and make place for Him. In His presence, we come to know our identity. There it is told us that we are made in His image, fallen into sin but redeemed through the blood of Christ and recreated in His glorious image. In the presence of the Almighty, we sense that we are new creatures through Christ. None of this can happen except God be present and actively working in us.

I have a good friend who is fond of saying that ideally a man should walk through life with one eye upon the things which make up his outer world and his other eye figuratively turned completely inward to continually scan his inner world. This is good advice but I have suggested an improvement to him. If it were possible to reconstruct our ocular anatomy, I would have one eye revolving, constantly sweeping the inner and outer worlds. The other eye would be fixed and steady upon God because the revelation of our real identity will come through our encounter with Him and His Word revealed to us.

Something else, however, needs to be added. We have said nothing about the need for people in our search for a Christian identity. Fellow believers play a crucial role in this search, as we will see.

Chapter Six
The Search for the Soul

EACH TUESDAY afternoon in the hospital where I am chaplain, about ten people gather with me to form a Bible study group – but we don't call it that. I like the name the group selected. We call ourselves "The Searchers." The purpose of our meeting is to search the Scriptures and ourselves simultaneously. Each time a new patient joins our group we explain why we call ourselves "The Searchers."

A few days ago a new patient asked us some very upsetting questions. He asked, "For *what* are you searching the Bible and yourselves? What do you hope to find? What will end your search?" This new man really set us to thinking.

I thought to myself of the famous psychiatrists (Jung, Horney, Maslow, Sullivan) who had addressed themselves to these very questions. Their writings about the search for the self had always impressed me as brilliant, but not the answer. They tell us that each human being is in search of his self, his identity, his spirit (which is the term I prefer), his person – call the essence of man what you will.

This search for the self can be seen very clearly in the lives of people we call transients. A transient is always on the go — from New York to Chicago; when the weather gets cold to Miami, then the West Coast; around the country and back, never sinking roots, "always itching" as these men put it. I once asked a transient-friend of mine what he was searching for and he replied, "I don't really know, but when I walk down the street I look for it; when I read a newspaper I search for it; when I go to a movie I expect to see it — but never do. Please don't ask me what 'it' is. I don't know."

We know what is operating in this man. He has lost his sense of being a person, of being a self, and he has externalized this internal problem on his world. By that I mean that he is really in search of his soul, but not finding it, he transposes this inward problem into an outward search for "the right town" or "the right job" — which, unfortunately, he never finds. Do you see the cleverness of the unconscious mind?

Our transient friend will remain unsatisfied, empty and very weary so long as he vainly tries to solve his problem by going from city to city. What will end his search? How will he ever find an answer for his life? Consider the following.

True encounter with persons — divine and human — produces self-discovery and fulfillment. Does that sound trite? Nothing I have said so far is more important or fundamental. Let me say it in a different way.

We *live* on persons. That sounds cannibalistic, I know, so let us first throw away that connotation. But not the idea, because we live on persons just as surely as we live on food and water. Our bodies need nourishment lest we die. No less do we all have the basic need to exist in and on the company of persons, and without such fellowship, we die a death more painful than physical death. It is the death of the person. Strangely, the body may continue to exist for years after the death of the person, in which case that person is a breathing corpse. This is the terrible tragedy we see in the transients. Their persons died for lack of reaching for and being replenished by other persons.

This is not to say that a "dead" person is no longer a human spirit. He is, but unto God and his fellow human beings he is dead. It is sin which causes this death of the person. Sin is like a cancer. We all have it. In some, the effects are not yet visible. In others, it is quite obvious that death is already at the door. Our desperate need for the healing of persons is universal.

Christ answers that need. "You he made alive, when you were dead through the trespasses and sins in which you once walked" (Ephesians 2:1). How does Christ make us alive? In a way which today offends us because it sounds cannibalistic. "He who eats my flesh and drinks my blood abides in me and I in him...so he who eats me will live because of me" (John 6:56,57). Living on the person of Jesus Christ, therefore, is basic and primary. Yet, since we are all members of His Body, we will need the persons of other Christians to give our spirits sustenance. We need *them* — not what they bring us, but them...and before them, Christ, our First Person.

In such a community of persons, one can feed his person. One may discover and fulfill his person in the dynamic meeting and creative dialogue which occurs in the genuine encounter with other persons. This creative meeting may be either painful or pleasurable; it may be quieting or fearful. The meeting may be in anger or peace, but it is always marked by a strong sense of emotional and personal engagement.

As examples, one could cite Jacob wrestling with the Angel of the Lord, Moses' call at the burning bush, Isaiah's vision of God in the temple. These were encounters with God. Through these meetings these men discovered themselves, their mission and, significantly, their people.

Most of us vainly try to avoid intense, close personal encounter because it is difficult for us to accept that our only ultimate good consists of other persons and our relationships to them. Instead of living on persons, we vainly try to make such things as our work, our power, our status, bring us self-discovery and fulfillment. The attempt never succeeds. Let us see an illustration of this.

I am thinking of a young man who wanted to be a minister. He was bright but immature when he graduated from seminary. Finally the goal of ordination was reached, but once he received it he felt empty and unfulfilled. The thought occurred to him that if he threw himself into his work he would find satisfaction. Even this did not suffice. Losing interest in his congregation, he undertook graduate study, but again, the moment he got his degree he knew that was not what he was seeking. The attempt to find identity and fulfillment through work had failed. We might call him a ministerial transient.

Our disillusioned pastor could also have tried power or positions of status in society but we can predict what would happen if he did. The soul does not come to self-consciousness through such things as ideas, things, work, power, education, money, sex, social status. We don't "have it made" when we have these. They all turn into dust if through them we seek the basic satisfactions of the soul. Only persons will do.

This is why, for example, godly mothers are often among the most satisfied people alive. Such a woman is oriented to people: her husband, her children, her God, her friends, the people in her church. A godly father can also find such personal fulfillment but often in our society the "cares of this world and the deceitfulness of riches" strongly entice him to things rather than persons. This temptation is a pact with the devil – the promise of much in return for a piece of one's soul. But the devil pays no one.

We are searching to become authentic, self-conscious persons. The lost is found when we "come to our*selves*" as the prodigal. The new life begins when we come into dialogue with Christ and the church with which He is identified. When we encounter Christ and these people who make up Christ's church, throwing our lot in with them, we cannot remain souls lost to ourselves.

Chapter Seven
Names Are Important

WHAT WE NAME a human spirit is of considerable importance. I would like to look with you in this chapter at some of the names we hang on people.

It was Dale Carnegie who taught us that the sweetest sound in all the world to another person is his name. We were advised to repeat a person's name often if we wanted to win friends and influence people. It followed that the worst error one could make was to mispronounce, misspell or forget the name of a new acquaintance.

We all desire to have people remember our name, speak it correctly and spell it the way we like it spelled. Many of us who have a jaw-breaking surname are saddled with a special problem, unless, of course, we change it—which you may consider doing if this applies to you. Just because one of our European ancestors jestingly complied with the order of Napoleon that all people must bear a surname is no reason why we and our descendants should struggle through the world with impossible surnames.

Leaving this matter of surnames, however, let us look at Christian names and their contamination by nicknames. Nicknames are usually diminutives. They begin in childhood and, hopefully, end when one reaches maturity. It is unfortunate that these nicknames are often carried over into the adult years with a meaning and function which is wholly inappropriate. I think it is a tragedy when a man in his middle years is still called "Buffalo" by his friends just because his playmates gave him that name while playing cowboys and Indians.

I plead for a return, in the case of adults, to the use of given Christian names because they give dignity and respect to our God-given persons.

Let us go on to talk about the use of title to designate certain persons in our society. What I have in mind here are titles such as Reverend, Doctor, Professor, Captain, or any others which have to do with our work.

I have no quarrel with these titles when one is involved in his particular work. But when I am on the beach with my friends, and above the noise of the crowd and the pounding surf I hear the shout, "Over here, Reverend, throw the ball over here!" I groan inwardly at such moments to lay aside my office and be treated as a person – as just plain Earl.

Do you know that there are people who feel uncomfortable as persons and prefer to be addressed and treated only in terms of their work? I once met a medical doctor at the YMCA. He was not my doctor, now was I his pastor. We had come to the Y to exercise and have fun. I introduced myself, using only my Christian name and surname because I wished to be a person to him, not a pastor. All this happened as he was dripping wet and draped in a towel. You would think that this would encourage a man to present himself to others simply as another human being who at times is all wet. Not my friend the doctor. "How do you do. I am Dr. Ernest Work. I am happy to meet you." I thought I detected a slight bow, but it was difficult to tell with that wet towel draped around him.

Turn now with me for a look at some parental names. The words *mother* and *father* are among the dearest names in the language when they are applied to our parents. Unfortunately, many parents from the time of their first child have called each other these names.

"Say, Mother, when are the children and I going to eat?" asks the husband of his wife.

"I don't know, Dad. Are you all washed and ready?" is the reply.

"Yes, Mother."

My friends who live this way tell me they do it out of habit; because of the children for whom they speak; because they like it; because their parents did it this way; because it is harmless; because there is nothing wrong with it. Their reasons leave me unimpressed. I flatly disagree with them. The real reason for these misnomers is that the marriage relationship has deteriorated to a point where the husband *feels* like his wife's son and the wife *feels* like a daughter to her husband.

We use whatever names we use on people for revealing reasons—not just out of habit or because they are handy names. We know too much about the operations of the unconscious mind to naively think that what we say has no meaning or rationale. When a man calls his wife "mother" he feels like a boy feels toward his mother. There is nothing wrong with that feeling in boys but it is wholly inappropriate in a mature man. Let a wife be respected and honored often by the dignity of her Christian name — the name which always reminds her that she is a unique person in God's world.

Christian men and women, of all people, ought to be concerned about the names given people to identify their persons. All persons are precious because they bear the image of God. Therefore they should be well named.

Let us remember that what we call a person indicates how we think of him. God has given us the highest honor in being called sons and daughters of the living God. This makes us brothers and sisters of the Son of God. Now if God thought so highly of us as His children, we ought to honor the people in our world by giving them names which befit their dignity as persons.

Part II
The New Identity
Through Christ

Chapter Eight
"The Truth Will Make You Free"

TRUTH IS the close agreement between a description of an object and what that object really is. I say you are holding a book in your hand. You agree. We both say: That is the truth. If I say you are holding a bouquet of flowers instead of this book, I speak a lie. My mind is then in bondage to a delusion. A delusion is a false opinion. It is a fantasy. Ideas and words which really describe reality are the truth.

Jesus spoke so truthfully in revealing His Father to us that He spoke of Himself as the truth personified: "I am...the truth."

Truth and reality always go together.

All else is delusion, fantasy, sin.

Sin is also a violation of God's law.

God's law has one loving intent: to lead us away from delusional thinking. We are commanded not to worship many gods because this is a delusion. The truth is that there is only one God. We are commanded to honor our parents because it is a delusion to think that we owe them nothing for all their care of us. The truth is that we are forever indebted to them. We are commanded not to steal because it is a delusion to pretend that something is ours when it really is not. The truth is that we own only what we earn through honest labor.

If we could keep God's law perfectly, we would be delusion-free. This explains why the poet in Psalm 119 never tires of exulting in the law of God. "I love thy commandments above gold, above fine gold" (verse 127). It was not the law as a purely legal instrument which gave him joy. The law was a guide to truth, reality and God. It still is. The problem of our inability to perfectly keep the law was decisively solved on a Tree by the Truth.

Our Lord told us that the truth would make us *free*. What is this freedom?

Real freedom is the reward of living truthfully. The choice to live a lie, to live untruthfully, to live a delusion, brings us into bondage.

Freedom, of course, never means license in the Scriptures. To live in disregard of God's laws inevitably means the bondage of the person. It is quite immaterial whether one is caught and punished. This is because the bondage is mainly internal.

But freedom is also internal. Freedom of the kind we have in mind here is freedom to really be the human being God created and re-created us to be. It is freedom to be, to exist with joy and a godly pride in a new identity through Christ.

Listen to the joy of Paul: "For freedom Christ has set us free"! We are in bondage to no man, no thing, no sin. We are free to be "bond-servants" only to One who will have us as no other than his joint-heirs! That is *freedom.* "If the Son makes you free, you will be free indeed," said our Lord.[1]

The truth frees people. I recall how I first really learned about this.

Several years ago I shared a hotel room with a fellow minister. In the morning we left our room, each carrying his own luggage. My friend carried only an attaché case. I carried two suitcases, a typewriter and an umbrella.

When my colleague offered to help me carry my luggage, I assured him rather grandiloquently that I was doing fine and needed no help. Even when his kind offer was repeated as we trudged up a steep hill, I grandly waved him away from my increasingly oppressive burden, choosing to remain in my splendid self-sufficiency. By the time we reached the top of that hill, I was so out of breath that I had to stop for a rest.

At that moment my companion also stopped and, while I stood there panting and perspiring, he delivered one of the most helpful yet devastating sermons I have ever heard!

"You!" he shouted. "You deluded preacher! You proud, self-sufficient man!" And after that bold introduction, he pointed out the truth to me. The *truth* was that I needed help with the luggage but was so enslaved to my pride that I would not ask for it. The *truth* was that I was a finite, human creature, not the 10-ton derrick of my delusions. Moreover, the truth was that other Christians needed opportunities to express their love by helping those in need — a fact I was unwilling to see.

[1] Galatians 5:1; John 3:36.

I tell you, it did not take me long to leave the world of my delusions and enter God's real world! We split the luggage and walked off.

My brother spoke the truth and by it, freed me from the bondage of my sin.

"The truth will make you free."

Now I feel we are ready to come to the point of this chapter. *Jesus Christ speaks such bold and accurate words to our sinful condition that we are stripped of all our delusions, pretenses and deceptions.*

He sees us as we really are. We are a long way off from God, detached and isolated from Him by sin which, according to its own peculiar law, separates persons.

One of my parishioners put it this way: "You can't be with God and stay a phony!" Many times my people communicate the truth much better than I do.

You and I—phonies? It is not easy to face the fact that we have set up our lives in such a way that it has become necessary to hide much of them. We have become masters of concealment and not infrequently, duplicity—trying to be two people.

You do not need to ask what that does to our identity. It splits it into two identities—the good guy whom we present to our fellows and the sinner whom we keep locked up in our secret, inner world. The former is what we could be but are not. The latter is what we are but need not be.

We become very skillful, after years of practice, in concealing our sins and broadcasting our virtues. This is exactly the opposite of what our Lord taught us. He often makes the point that we should conceal our virtues (fasting, prayers, mercy, etc.) and confess our faults openly. O. Hobart Mowrer makes the interesting and valid point that we become what we conceal. Whatever is hidden in our hearts has a way of forming our self-concept. As a pastor I can testify that the people who give me most problems are not those who quite obviously have fallen into sin but are the nice, respectable people. Their sins are carefully locked within. No wonder they feel like sinners! But let that person conceal his virtures, exposing his faults to his fellows and God, and on the promise of our Lord, he will sense in himself a new identity.

But not so fast. This is not accomplished by agreeing that this is a fine idea. Think carefully about the price of this new identity. It hurts to pay the price. It means the death of sin in us and the birth of Truth.

But if we buy it, the Truth will make us free. I mean really free.

Chapter Nine
Repentance

THE WORD FOR repentance in the New Testament is *metanoia* and it literally means "change of mind." It is the key word in the message of John the Baptist and our Lord spoke of it frequently. His parable of the prodigal son is a brilliant illustration of a man who in great sorrow repented of his sins and returned to his father's home. All believers see themselves in the prodigal son in whom a godly grief produced a repentance which led to salvation.

How are we led to repent in this modern age?

There may have been a day when people repented because the preacher shouted: Repent! Unfortunately for us modern preachers, we find that this repels most people today. People complain that it leaves them completely unmoved. Rather than feeling any sense of sorrow about their lives, they feel judged and rejected by the word *repent*.

I must confess that if I approached my hospital parishioners with the command to repent, they would leave me. And yet, as their pastor, I know that if there is anything which my people need it is a "godly grief" and a "change of mind" which will steer them away from the road to disaster and turn them back to God. How, then, shall we approach these people?

I have no final answers but I would like to share with you my approach. Though I am a pastor, every Christian can employ this approach for it is almost absurdly simple.

I simply attempt to speak the truth and face the facts. Please note that I say "attempt" for no man has a hold on ultimate truth, nor do any of us know all the facts about a person. But this should not deter us from an effort to state the truth in the manner and spirit of Jesus in John 4. The Samaritan woman whom Jesus encountered at the well was a person whose greatest need was for someone to be truthful with her. Our Lord confronted her with a number of falsehoods in her life.

First, she was too pre-occupied with the water in the well, so Christ turned her attention to the water of eternal life—the true water. This was followed by a bold suggestion to take an honest look at the sin of her life: "Go, call your husband" (4:16). When she denied having one, our Lord gave her a little more truth to think about. He told her she was a mistress to a number of men. This was such strong medicine that she began talking about some theological issues in order to evade Jesus, but even in this discussion, our Lord held up the truth to her.

It was in imitation of Jesus' counseling technique that I dealt, lately, with an alcoholic parishioner who was speaking of the recent death of his wife. A part of our conversation went like this—

PASTOR: Sounds like something you cannot accept — that your wife is gone.

JOHN: Well, I guess I'll *have* to accept it.

PASTOR: Oh no, you can fight it, oppose it, resent it — you can go to your grave feeling that a terrible injustice has been done to you.

JOHN: But I don't *want* to feel that way.

PASTOR: If you really mean that, surrender your wife to God. (We left this subject and began talking about his alcoholism.)

JOHN: I guess I just drank a little too much after her death. That's my only problem.

PASTOR: The problem is not that you just drank a little too much. You are an alcoholic. The only way to save your life now is never to drink again. Have you made peace with that fact?

JOHN: Not quite. You see, I only drink to take up the void after my wife died. I plan to cut down and gradually avoid alcohol.

PASTOR: You do not accept the fact of your alcoholism. We disagree with you. You were on our critical list when you arrived here. Our doctors say you are in the latter stages of alcoholism.

Obviously, my approach is not calculated to accept John's feelings; nor do I intend that he should feel better because of what I have said to him. As a matter of fact, it made him feel very much worse. Whether or not he feels worse or better is not my concern. My task is to help the man.

I should also add that I am not interested in first of all making him feel ashamed or sorry for what he has done. No pastor has the right to make another man feel guilty. If these feelings come about in the person seeking help, his own conscience will have to be his accuser.

If my reasoning is correct, it follows that we should not attempt to bring people to repentance by pointing out how they have violated the Law of God or, for that matter, any part of the Scriptures. I do not believe people are brought to Christ by such legalistic methods. "Throwing the Book" at a sinner is precisely what the self-righteous Pharisees loved to do and you recall our Lord's treatment of them. We Christians have no business manipulating people in such a way that they feel sorry and guilty for violating a Book, infallible though it is.

If true repentance comes, it will come out of the anguished realization that one is *leading a life of falsehood,* or as one man expressed it, "seeing how phony I was." Falsehood becomes known when a "fool for Christ" has concern and enough courage to let some light of truth shine upon falsehood. The word of truth to my alcholoic parishioner is not a quotation from the Law which says "thou shalt not kill" but a statement that John is alcoholic even when he denies it.

I simply let John live with some truth for a few days. The Holy Spirit—Who works where and when He pleases—led John to an agonizing confrontation with himself which issued in a deep sense of guilt. He experienced guilt not only for specific sins but also for having mislived his life in such a way that it represented, in its totality, a massive violation of God's intention for his life.

A young boy, who lived on a very isolated farm, once went to his father with a request to see the circus coming into town. The father was glad to give his boy the opportunity to have a little fun and be among people. The lad was given four dollars with instructions to first get a haircut and then see the circus.

As the boy sat waiting in the barber shop, a loud commotion was heard out on the street. It was the circus parade! Everyone, including the barber, ran out of the shop and watched the colorful circus people and their stage animals. It was a fantastic parade! The boy loved every minute of it and was thrilled to pieces. But too soon the end of the circus was in sight and the last one in the parade was an uproariously funny clown who delighted the boy no end.

As the clown was passing, the lad stepped over to him and asked nervously, "Who do I pay?"

"Me," said the clown. And with that the boy gave the clown three dollars. The clown took it and walked off.

The boy went back to the barber and, upon having his hair cut, went home, satisfied that he had seen the circus.

Not until sometime later did he discover that he had missed the whole show!

My parishioner, John, felt this way about his life, a life which had been mislived for 34 years and he did not even know it! He had missed the whole show. What a colossal mistake!

In the chapter to follow, we examine the nature of the guilt which issues from such a realization.

Chapter Ten
Guilt

GUILT IS both a legal status and a feeling which results when law has been violated.

When we have broken the law, our legal status is one of being punishment-worthy.

But how shall we describe the *feeling* of guilt? I believe its basic ingredient is an anxious anger directed against oneself. This is why guilt is such an uncomfortable feeling. We shall return to a consideration of this feeling, but first let us look more closely at the state of guilt.

God has put His law in the world. The violation of this law we call sin, which in turn entails guilt. That law is ubiquitous — it is written in our hearts, built into our consciences, spelled out in the Scriptures, reflected in our courts of law, and established eternally in the heavens. It is an inspiring and wonderful thing to contemplate, as the Psalmist taught us in Psalm 119.

We violate that law. Let me point out, however, that this simple statement is something which only a person of faith can admit and accept. The irreligious contend that guilt is not a status before law but *merely* a feeling, and one, moreover, which is best ignored. I must admit that the irreligious man is logically consistent. If God and His law are ignored, it follows that the state and feeling of guilt are ignorable.

My point here is that our guilt is *real.* We have it because we have sinned. Our sins – the evil words spoken, our murderous hatreds, our adultery either in the heart or in act, our deceptions, our countless idolatries – all rise up against us to bedevil us with guilt, the reality of which we are only too keenly aware, if we believe.

But let us now look at the *feeling* of guilt.

The purpose of God's law is to preserve our lives. When we become destructive toward persons (ourselves, or others) through sin, we feel anxiety. Anxiety is the threat to one's very being (Tillich). We can understand that this, in turn, would create that feeling of acute displeasure which we call anger. Notice that with guilt, anger is directed toward ourselves. It is self-condemning; it vents its fury upon the guilty self in an attempt to make him pay the full price for his transgression.

We see, therefore, that there is no mercy in our feelings of guilt. Our guilt lives by the *lex talionis* (the law of retaliation). "The sinner must pay in full" is its motto. If one is destructive toward himself or another person, the sinner must be punished, says our guilty conscience.

The guilty person understandably seeks means of ridding himself of his damning guilt. Most people seek to do this on their own terms and by their own methods. We might call this the do-it-yourself method of guilt disposal because what is attempted is self-atonement. Let us turn to the life of a person known to most of us and possibly learn from him the destructive operation of guilt and the futility of self-atonement.

I speak of Jack Ruby – the man who killed Lee Oswald, the assassin of President John Kennedy. The full facts of his life may never be known but the picture that emerges at this point is of a man who lived on the edge of the underworld. He was also the owner of a night-club business whose specialty was burlesque. Jack lived in the entertainment world, and even in such little ways as selling "twist boards," he lived to give people pleasure and fun. We know also that he was a nominal adherent to the Jewish Faith. The general impression I get is a picture of a pleasure-oriented life burdened with considerable amounts of unattended guilt.

After Lee Oswald shot President Kennedy, Jack Ruby began to make plans – plans which had a self-atoning character. Perhaps they were unconscious, perhaps conscious; nonetheless they were plans for which he is responsible. He decided to kill the killer of President Kennedy. Why? Did he not know that the law would deal with Oswald? Surely he did. Did he not know he would surely be caught? Of course. Was he insane? I doubt it very much. To understand why, we must look at what the murder of Oswald might do for Jack Ruby, particularly on an unconscious level.

For Jack Ruby, the murder of Oswald was a "good" act. Remember that after his capture, Ruby's immediately given reason for the murder was that he could not bear the thought of Mrs. Kennedy's coming back to Dallas to bear the ordeal of a long court trial against Lee Oswald. Now was not that a laudable motive for which all America would rise up to bless him?

This reasoning was, of course, absurd. I suspect, however, that the need for atonement from guilt was so strong in the life of this man that his deluded mind actually chose the murder of a murderer as a way of making himself justified unto himself.

I believe also that Jack Ruby knew that he would die if he killed Oswald. This consequence could only have unconscious appeal to a man so guilt-ridden. For him to die would simply mean that he was getting "what he had coming." So how could he lose?

Religiously, I suggest that the whole episode of Jack Ruby and his crime is an illustration to us of the results of leaving accumulated guilt unattended, and the insanity of self-atonement devices. These are some of the lessons for us to learn. If we learn them, Jack Ruby's life, even in its most tragic moments, will be of benefit to us.

I recall from a newspaper account that Jack Ruby felt he could not over-estimate the effect of the Bible upon his thinking while awaiting trial. Could it be that at that late hour, Jack Ruby was abandoning the idea of self-atonement and was coming to terms with Jesus Christ who made atonement for the sin of the world? I pray so. Our Lord, you know, is practiced in saving dying criminals.

Chapter Eleven
Kinds of Atonement

HERE, IN GENERAL, is what we mean by atonement – it is the amending satisfaction given for wrongdoing. When we use the word theologically, it refers to the effect of Jesus' suffering and death in redeeming mankind and bringing about the reconciliation of God to man. Atonement is the means for disposing of man's guilt.

There are three kinds of atonement in the world today. The first two kinds are absolutely false, not to mention ineffective. The third type of atonement is Christ's. His is absolutely trustworthy, totally effective.

The first type of atonement is the attempt of man to reconcile himself to God by means of good works. Paul spent a good part of the New Testament debunking this impertinent idea. Perhaps his classic statement is Ephesians 2:8,9: "For by grace you have been saved through faith; and this is not your own doing, it is the gift of God – not because of works, lest any man should boast." A passage such as this flatly rules out the possibility of using good works as a device to atone for our guilt. The Scriptures are so plain on this matter that it is unnecessary to dwell on it at length.

The second kind of atonement devised by man is the self-destructive type. This is clearly seen in mental illnesses, but all of us use it in varying degrees. Actually, we would do better to speak of such illnesses as being in the area of our emotions or feelings rather than in the mind itself. Illness on the level of emotionality manifests itself by such things as agonizing anxiety, overpowering fears, destructive rage, repetitive acts which we find difficult to control, the cessation of rational thoughts and speech, suicidal tendencies, frightening bizarre thoughts. These are some of the major ways in which the feelings become ill. Notice that in every symptom mentioned here, the purpose seems to be to say or do something to break down or even destroy the person.

What *is* that destructive force in the person? I agree with O. Hobart Mowrer *(The Crisis in Religion and Psychiatry)* that the great destroyer in people is their guilt. All people have guilt and are struggling for ways to dispose of it, one of which is through mental illness.

Let us take just one of the symptoms to demonstrate how a person may attempt to deal with his guilt by means of a do-it-yourself method of atonement which issues in self-destruction. Look at a person who performs repetitive acts which he finds difficult to control. He washes his hands incessantly – perhaps five times after touching anything dead, etc. Certain words, certain songs keep racing through his brain. He is deathly afraid of stepping on the cracks in the side-walk and he is terrified by the sight of dog excrement near him as he walks along the street.

Most psychiatrists are convinced that such a person is struggling with the problem of guilt. Compulsive rituals are his crude, ineffective means of atoning for his guilt. If he washes his hands the prescribed number of times, he is freed from his feelings of guilt — maybe. But even if the *feeling* is released, the guilt itself remains to plague him again.

Small wonder, then, that Erich Fromm has defined neurosis as a "private form of religion."[1] This is precisely the case. A neurosis or psychosis (which is a more extreme form of emotional illness) is a do-it-yourself religion calculated to deal with the fundamental problem in the heart of every human being — guilt. The pity and tragedy of it all is that these self-atonement devices succeed only in greater self-destruction.

Another way of self-destruction by means of self-atonement is through what we commonly know as physical illness. I need not go into great detail about this because you can easily understand what I mean if we talk about ulcers.

Ulcers mean that a man cannot "stomach" certain feelings he has about his world. There are many guesses as to what these indigestible feelings are — anger, over-dependency, fear, resentment, jealousy, etc. Notice how these feelings usually have an outward object as their target. For example, as a rule we resent *something,* we are afraid of *someone,* or are jealous of *another person.* These feelings, with the exception of self-directed anger, leave the producer of

[1] *Psycholanalysis and Religion* (New Haven, Conn. Yale University Press, 1950), p. 27.

the feelings in good shape. But now add guilt to this man's feelings and we notice that he instinctively begins to rid himself of it by making himself the target of his self-destructive guilt. Yet, no one with a healthy mind will consciously attack himself, so the unconscious mind takes over and produces a socially acceptable illness, an ulcer in this case. The ulcer serves as the punishment for guilt. The ulcer "atones" for guilt through our own suffering. But this is not God's will, for He abhors our do-it-yourself atonement devices and points us to the perfect atonement of His Son.

This is not the signal, however, for healthy people to incriminate people suffering from ulcers or other physical illnesses. A man may be born with a weak stomach which would quickly react to the stress of even small amounts of tension over guilt. Remember, too, the words of our Lord: "Let him who is without sin among you, be the first to throw a stone at her" (John 8:7).

There is yet another self-destructive atonement device under this second type which I will only mention. It is to work out feelings of guilt upon society. This is the way of the criminal who eventually is caught and then atones for his guilt by living for years in a prison. Though he may be sent to prison only for one transgression, we may be quite sure that on the unconscious level, the criminal feels that imprisonment or death is the just recompense for the whole of his dissolute life. (Cf. the analysis of Jack Ruby in chapter 10.) The criminal's particular crime for which he is sent to prison or death is usually only an ironic, perverted kind of face-saver.

God's way of disposing of our guilt is the atonement made by Christ. Christ's atonement was foreshadowed in the countless animals slaughtered for sacrifice through the Old Testament period. The fundamental issue with which both Old and New Testaments deal is guilt.

"The Lamb of God, who takes away the sin of the world," went to Calvary and "when Christ had offered for all time a single sacrifice for sins, he sat down at the right hand of God."[2] *How* is this accomplished? you ask. May I be frank with you? I think you have asked the wrong question. You ask about the mechanics of God's salvation. Not even our best theologians can answer your question. But would you change your question to this — Could I simply trust God to rid me of guilt according to *His* means of atonement? God's instrument is Christ and though we cannot spell out exactly *how* His atonement works, we have compelling proof that it does. The proof is a deep, abiding sense of forgiveness within us.

Our guilt, we were saying, is disposed by transfer (imputation) to the sacrificial innocent victim, Christ Jesus. Nothing in all the world is more needful or practical than this kind of salvation from sin. It is almost as if God is shouting to us: "I plead with all men to discard all self-atonement devices! They are ruining you, my creatures. Make a good confession. Repent of your sins but leave the matter of atonement to Me. I have provided a way. Your part is to continue the struggle against sin — but not to deal with past sins, past guilt. I want you to live!

[2] John 1:29; Hebrews 10:12.

I can testify to you as a person and a pastor that this Way brings peace to the war between the conscience and the sinner; this Way brings release to energies which were formerly tied up with do-it-yourself atonement schemes; this Way brings a serene joy to depressed and despairing human spirits.

And, best of all, it is through this Way that Christ forms a new identity in us. We become new creatures in Christ.

We now see ourselves not as the scum of the earth, nor as self-righteous saints, but as people—just people, beloved of God, loving other people and delighting in the gift of life.

> Thou hast multiplied, O Lord my God,
>   thy wondrous deeds and thy thoughts toward us;
>   none can compare with thee!
>   *—Psalm 40:5*

Chapter Twelve
A Christian Identity

A YEAR BEFORE Mr. Cain became a Christian, he was sitting in a tavern on his fourth martini, growing more eloquent as a conversationalist with each drink. Then he happened to use the word "perrogative."

"You said it wrong," reported the man on the next barstool. "It is prerogative, not perrogative."

Mr. Cain was sure of his ground. "Go back to school, fella. In this country it is perrogative." This was the opening gun of what turned out to be a young war. Each man boldly asserted his absolute infallibility in spelling the word under debate. Additional doses of alcohol were of no help in cooling the friction between these linguistic authorities. Indeed, it was like throwing gasoline on fire. They were at the point of blows when their genial bartender suggested they settle the argument with a dictionary. A novel suggestion.

Mr. Cain returned from the drug-store with an abridged pocket-dictionary. In the presence of his opponent, the book was solemnly opened to...prerogative. Cain had lost! But not so fast! He protests— that the *un*abridged edition will support him!

There are people who believe they cannot be wrong. Mr. Cain was one of them for he cherished a picture of himself as the Errorless Man. This crazy picture was who he thought he was! When Mr. Cain asked the question: "What kind of an I am I?" this image of himself as Mr. Infallibility was a large part of the answer. It was his concept of his identity.

I say his *concept* of his identity, but not his identity itself, for this cannot be conceptualized. The reason for this is quite apparent. Man's existential identity can no more be conceptualized than the being of God. God is divine spirit, a reality which evades capture by human thoughts and ideas. Man is made in God's spiritual image and is fully as nondefinable as God. Ideas about and feelings of spirits can be conceptualized but not man's identity as a human spirit.

Let us leave these rather philosophical reflections and begin to spell out what might be the concept of a person's identity if he is a Christian? We saw our friend Cain as Mr. Infallibility. Now let us see him as Mr. Christian. Notice three things about a Christian identity.

First, a Christian sees himself positioned *under* God and *with* people. Recall how Mr. Cain formerly thought of himself as above his drinking companion— above, in the sense that Cain had superior knowledge and a monopoly on the truth. The moment one thinks of himself as above people, he plays god. This has the effect of dethroning the true God and making a god out of oneself. What a tragedy! The world of Mr. Cain was all out of kelter because he was not properly positioned in it.

I know of a young woman who is alcoholic and much distressed because of it. She has a friend who suggested she see me. Her response was violent: "Go to hell. I can't stand these pious ministers. Besides, I believe in God so why should I go to this minister?" Our alcoholic woman feels she has superior knowledge to her friend. There is a feeling of aboveness in her, and what she sorely needs is a sense of withness. If she were truly with people, she would be under God. Perhaps someday, pray God, she will learn through Alcoholics Anonymous to submit to a Power higher than herself and become interdependent (rather than independent or over-dependent) in relationship to people. The day in which she becomes properly positioned in the world, will be the day she will realize at least a part of her Christian identity.

The second mark of a Christian identity is that one sees himself, without humiliation or degradation, as the object of God's grace. It is hardly necessary to demonstrate that we are needy creatures. In fact, our neediness is so complete that we are totally dependent upon God to lift us out of sin. In the fullest sense, "we are *his* [God's] workmanship, created in Christ Jesus for good works" (Ephesians 2:10). We exist only by grace. If God had not had mercy on us, both in creating and recreating us, we would not be. John Bunyan captured the idea when, pointing to a derelict, he said: "There, but for the grace of God, go I."

This information shatters the image of ourselves as self-sufficient. We can no longer see ourselves as independent, autonomous and self-saved people, for we know this is not our true identity but a product of our delusional thinking. Our true identity is found only in the presence of the living, loving God. As we stand before Him, we come to know ourselves as people who have fallen into a pit from which we cannot extricate ourselves.

When Isaiah saw a vision of God, he cried out: "Woe is me! For I am lost; for I am a man of unclean lips and I dwell in the midst of people of unclean lips" (Isaiah 6:5). Isaiah could not have had this experience until God presented Himself to him. Recall our friend, Mr. Cain, who lived in a world in which God had no place. Cain could have looked at himself endlessly and never seen anything but his "omniscience." The moment God was cut into his world, he immediately sensed his basic sin—pride.

That was shocking enough, but additionally Mr. Cain realized that he could not be saved from his sin unless God would do it. It is a terribly helpless feeling to realize that one cannot handle the consequence of his own deeds. But in that moment of great despair, the Holy Spirit did not fail Mr. Cain. The Holy Spirit recreated him in the image of Christ, or, we might better say, the identity of Christ. Mr. Cain now sees himself as an object of God's grace and the recipient of a new humanity.

A Christian identity involves something else, in the third place, which is very difficult to explain. Let us begin with the rather clumsy statement and then proceed to refine it. *The kind of person a Christian is, is an authentically human person.*

That word *human* has a connotation of weakness with which I do not wish to tamper. It is a necessary part of our humanity, even our new humanity. One of the most important pieces of wisdom which Mr. Cain possesses, is the knowledge that he is weak. He knows he is too weak to go into certain towns where old memories and new temptations shake him up. Cain, who now admits to being an alcoholic, knows he is too weak to sit drinking Coca-Cola with old friends in a nearby tavern. He is also too weak not to need all that Alcoholics Anonymous offers; so, night after night, like all the other recovered alcoholics, he attends their meetings.

There is, however, also a connotation of warmth and goodness in the word *human*. And surely, one who has a new identity through Christ is the loving person God intended him to be. In my mind, this Christian person of whom I am speaking is characterized by an openness, a non-defensiveness which allows him to communicate to others sizeable amounts of the basic Christian attitudes – faith, hope and love. It is almost as if these qualities spontaneously radiate from him.

As I write about this elusive quality of humanness in people, I find my thoughts gravitating toward the Christ, for if anyone was ever authentically human, it was He. It is for this good reason that the Scriptures present Him to us as the model after which we are to fashion our identities. This was the thrilling message which Paul sent to the early church. Listen to him.

> For those whom he foreknew he also predestined to be conformed to the image of his Son, in order that he might be the first-born among many brethren (Romans 8:29).

> And we all, with unveiled face, beholding the glory of the Lord, are being changed into his likeness from one degree of glory to another; for this comes from the Lord who is the Spirit (II Corinthians 3:18).

Understand, however, that a Christian identity is a goal which, through the power of God, we seek to fulfill. It is a long struggle and at times we feel like questioning the wisdom of our Lord in giving us only threescore and ten years to work at it. The foundation has been laid once for all time through the atoning work of Christ, but our sanctification is slow and arduous because we keep finding things in us which do not conform to the image of Christ.

The next six chapters examine a few of the attitudes which oppose the new man in us. I have selected a few feelings which we do not like to find in us, such as fear, censoriousness, neurotic guilt, morbid self-depreciation and double-mindedness. (There are many more, but this book is to be only one volume.)

Part III
Finding Some Things
In Us
We Do Not Like

Chapter Thirteen
"I Am Afraid"

FOR THE SAKE OF clarity, let us sharply distinguish the terms *anxiety, fear* and *dread* as they are used in our culture.

Anxiety is a deep feeling of uneasiness caused by the "threat of non-being" (Tillich). In other words, it is an uncomfortable sensation that something evil might soon happen which will harm if not destroy oneself. Unfortunately, the sources of anxiety are difficult to locate and the ultimate consequence is also unknown. When we are anxious, we just know that something is wrong but we cannot say why, what or whereunto it is wrong.

Fear is similar to anxiety in that we sense that something dreadful is going to happen to us. The difference between them is that with fear the source is known. For example, we fear a war, or illness, or an auto accident. You can see that fear is a bit easier to deal with than anxiety simply because one can get at it.

Dread is close to the idea of panic. The fear and its accompanying anxiety is so great that we are "floored." The Roman soldiers guarding the tomb on

Easter morning are good examples because they "became as dead men."

In this chapter, we are concerned with *fear*. Most everyone would agree that *fear is an emotion which occurs when a person senses a rising danger*. Whether that danger exists in reality or fantasy makes no difference to the person who is afraid. He understands all too well the discomfort of this feeling which tells him the frightening news that his life is in danger! For, after all, is not this the message which fear always brings? In the Cuban crises of 1962, we were afraid both that Russia was preparing to launch a missile attack and also that our quarantine of Cuba would lead to thermonuclear war. We feared that in either case we might be killed. We can see clearly now that it was a good thing we *were* afraid! Our fear caused us to say *nyet* to the Cuban missile bases, and here at home we began to take seriously the advice of our civil defense officials. A good number of us packed a box of food and placed it in the cellar. This was because the danger was real. When danger is real, it is appropriate and wise to respond to fear, for it causes us to take steps which will preserve our lives.

A good number of our fears, however, do not come from real situations in our environment but from our inner world of fantasy. I know of a person who went through months of agony just because of illusory fear. He had developed a little wart on his arm and was sure he had cancer. A medical doctor gave him tests, assured him that this wart was not cancerous and that it was nothing to worry about as long as it did not grow. The patient was not at all pleased with the report. He was *sure* he had cancer and the proof of it was right on his arm! In a couple of weeks, he felt, he would have dozens of these bumps and soon he would be dying of cancer all because of this careless doctor.

It is obvious that the patient's inner world of fantasy meant more to him than the real world. Why this is so is not always easy to see. It is obvious to one trained in dealing with people, however, that this cancer-fantasy is just a convenient peg on which to hang a deep desire to punish oneself by feeling miserable for some reason totally unrelated to cancer. The real cause of the fear, though concealed in the unconscious mind, would appear to have something to do with guilt. Guilt always seeks atonement, either through our Lord's perfect atonement or by "taking it out" on ourselves in some destructive manner. What breaks us down, makes life bitter, and even destroys us, better than the burden of unrelieved guilt and fear? Only the accomplished redemption of the Saviour of the world can give us release from our guilt and restore us. Self-atonement attempts to justify us to ourselves fail miserably. We need nothing less than a pardon from the Ultimate One in the universe – our God in Jesus Christ.

There is one thing about this patient, however, which we should not fail to appreciate. It is that his fear-feeling is real and that he is in pain. The only thing unreal is this delusion about cancer.

Since the feeling of fear, whether based on reality or fantasy, is real, the problem we face is how to handle it. You notice I do not say that the problem is to get rid of it. Sometimes one can diminish fear by a close study of the facts, but even then there is the fear which is justified by the facts. Moreover, since fear is a constantly recurring phenomenon and of such value to us at times, it is best to learn how to live with it.

Remember first, that we are not our feelings. We are human spirits who have fears but *are not* fear itself. This drawing of a line between who we are as created beings and what we feel is most crucial because it is impossible to get leverage on the feeling unless there is an "I" distinguished from the feeling.

You may find my second suggestion a bit strange. It is this—consider our great need of making a full confession to God in the presence of another person. We Protestants have a terrible blind spot on this matter of confession. It is true that priests and pastors cannot forgive sins. Only God can do that. But a listening third party can surely help us to be honest to God and if only we were that, both our actual guilt and our neurotic fears would leave us. For neurotic fear (i.e., groundless, inappropriate fear) is the result of free-floating guilt which, because it is unconfessed and undealt with, attaches itself to randomly chosen, innocent objects in our environment and then screams a disturbing promise of calamity to us as the just reward for our guilt.

And finally, consider God's love as the antidote of fear. "There is no fear in love, but perfect love casts out fear" (I John 4:18). God's love is so perfect that not only is He love personified but all thought of judgment and punishment toward us are impossible because the Son of God was the expiation for our sins. So we are God-loved and on this sure foundation we can lay all the burdensome fears which our environment places upon us. Nothing can ultimately hurt us if we are secure in the love of God. St. Paul, you may remember, asked himself whether such things as tribulation, distress, persecution, famine, nakedness, peril or sword would ever make him so fearful as to separate him from the love of God. "No," says Paul, "in all these things we are more than conquerors through him who *loved* us" (Romans 8:35,37).

May God's love conquer all fear in us. Our little children teach us how to do this. When a child is afraid, he flees to the protection of his mother and finds security in her love. Now nothing can really go wrong. Yet, sometimes a mother is a disappointment and the child is let down. It is because mothers are imperfect in their love.

God's love is true and perfect. It conquers fear, for God is love.

Chapter Fourteen
Censoriousness

DURING THE SUMMER of 1963, the newspapers were full of accounts concerning a chiropractor in England, Dr. Stephen Ward, who was the manager of a very high-priced prostitute named Christine Keeler. Miss Keeler rocked the entire British government by doing business with government officials from her own country as well as Russia. It was feared that Miss Keeler's customers were exchanging government secrets under the threat of black-mail. Miss Keeler and Dr. Ward were brought to court, found guilty, and were just about to be sentenced when Dr. Ward committed suicide.

The trial of Dr. Ward contains a lesson which our society needs to learn. The lesson I have in mind does not have to do with prostitution or living off the earnings of prostitutes. I refer to the evil of fault-finding on the part of the public. Dr. Ward in his suicide note was justified, I feel, in complaining that he was the victim of many "vultures." The manner in which the press sensationalized the testimony of each witness, and the way in which people throughout the land "enjoyed" the accounts is a testimony to the creeping moral paralysis particularly in England but also in this country.

Censoriousness is the habit of selecting an undeniable fault in another person and using it to cover up a multitude of similar sins in the faultfinder. Jesus spoke of faultfinding when he asked, "Why do you see the speck that is in your brother's eye, but do not notice the log that is in your own eye?" (Matthew 7:3).

Faultfinding differs radically from an unemotional, regretfully made estimate of another person based upon facts. It is entirely proper that Dr. Ward be brought to court and judged for his acts. Such is the law for every member of society. But why all the fanfare, the "oh's" and "aha's," the carping criticism, the self-righteous indignation and even sheer delight over what was done by Stephen Ward and Christine Keeler? You know why—because great masses of people would dearly love to do what they did but are restrained only by social pressure and are dreadfully unhappy about it!

The faultfinder has a neat way of setting up his world. First he looks at himself and tries to find a bit of virtue. He takes this one virtue and naively trusts that it will magically represent his entire character. As in TV westerns, he now wears a white hat—but *inside* rather than on top of his head. He is a "good guy." The next task is to find a peccadillo in a bad guy and give him a black hat. This neatly divides the world between good and bad people.

Such a division is a delusion. All people are different shades of gray including the late Dr. Ward. Witness the splendid use of his artistic and healing gifts.

Why is faultfinding so enjoyable? Because it

provides us with a temporary stay from making an honest self-inspection. The reprieve means a lot to us. The moment a sincere self-inspection begins, the fun is over because invariably we find that we are trumpeting our own secret faults. Tennyson was right when he said: "Dark is the world to thee; thyself art the reason." But that is strong medicine for any soul to take because we like to see others as sinners but not ourselves.

Yet the very sin we choose to see in others is usually the one that is giving us trouble. "We are prone to see in others our own unexplored tendencies. Some people who are over-concerned about the morals of the rising generation are fighting, no doubt, some of their own projected inclinations. The struggle *within* has determined their interest in things without."[1] Judas Iscariot's concern over the costliness of the ointment used on the Master's feet, is a classic example.

"But," someone says, "what if others really are at fault?" Then resist the temptation to appoint yourself judge. Reach out to help the one at fault but leave judgment in the hands of those appointed to the task: God, ecclesiastical authority, the civil magistrate and the individual's conscience.

Check also to see what is your attitude as you point out the fault. Granted, there is a time to speak to an erring person and possibly even take action against him as in the case of Dr. Ward. But check the spirit in which this is done. Is there a secret pleasure in it? Or are you reluctant and constrained to bring the facts to the attention of the person? If the latter, you are not faultfinding but concerned. The Old Testament prophets found many faults in their people but always with tears, invitations, promises and a matchless concern for people.

There is something else we may do. Edward Strecker once said: "The critics are rarely the creators — they often are the disappointed creators."[2] Creative people seldom criticize because they are up and doing constructive things. The critic, on the other hand, is a talker but not much of a doer. But this can change if the critic will concentrate on creativity within the circle of his ability.

We can also be helped in this problem of censoriousness by staying in close community with other Christians. One of the most dramatic and encouraging signs in the church today is the growth of the small group movement. Throughout our land, small groups of Christians are meeting for purposes of honest appraisal, spiritual discussion, confession and prayer. Dr. Sam Shoemaker pioneered in this field and his work is being carried on energetically by the Faith at Work organization. I am sure there are other groups of which I have no knowledge. Through small cell groups, many have been helped to see things more realistically and lovingly.

One fellow, a college student who was cynical and judgmental about everyone except himself, joined such a group in a church near his college. For the first time in his life, people were honest without being hostile. They told him he was unbearably censorious and acted like the judge of all the earth. It was hard to

[1] Edward A. Strecker and Kenneth E. Appel, *Discovering Ourselves (New York: The Macmillan Company, 1962), p. 217. Used by permission.*
[2] *Ibid.*, p. 218.

take but he took it and, praise God, made some changes. It can happen to all of us.

There is no better way to deal with the problem of censoriousness than to be in close dialogue with a group of Christians who dare to be honest with us.

Chapter Fifteen
The Subhuman Feeling

WE COME NOW to a problem in our lives which bedevils all of us and, worse, damages our Christian identity. It is the problem of feeling subhuman, seeing ourselves as inferior to others. Let us note three things about this common feeling.

Note first that the person who feels inferior is the one who judges himself inferior. Even if the people with whom I live tell me I am inferior, I must still choose whether to buy their opinion or not. Surely I cannot say that God tells me I am a subhuman person. We are all prone to sin, but we share equally the dignity of being made in God's image. So when I feel inferior, it is I who judge myself to be inferior to others.

Secondly, the *standard* of judgment we use to judge ourselves is invariably self-chosen and even worse, unscriptural. We go to the people who make up our world and using them as a standard, bring ourselves into judgment. At other times we go to the world of fantasy and draw out one of our idols to use as a standard. When one is presumptuous enough to make his own laws, appoint himself as his own judge and then hand himself a verdict of guilty, that person's life will be at once both a comedy and a tragedy.

Finally, if we are going to use this term inferiority, it is crucial that we determine just in which sense we can use it. Are you inferior as to *human* status? The answer is, of course not. You are a human being as well as I. If you are a business man and I a chaplain, does that mean I am occupationally inferior to you or you to me? No, it only means we do *different* things. But now let us suppose that we are both businessmen who are working at our full potential. Our work output may vary, but if we are both using our talents to the fullest, who would be so foolish as to argue that one of us is inferior to the other? We are just differently equipped. If I am the lowest producer and feel inferior at this point, it is no longer my inferiority complex which gives me trouble but either my jealousy or laziness. My work is then cut out for me.

We are now in position to see that whenever one complains of an inferiority complex, that person also has a superiority complex. Karen Horney in her book, *Neurosis and Human Growth*,[1] has brilliantly illustrated this as she describes the "despised image" and the "idealized image" which are always together in one and the same person. If you would like to confirm this, you need only recall the picture of a person who continually bemoans his depravity and worthlessness but at the very same time haughtily spurns the reception of God's forgiving grace in his life.

I recall a middle-aged woman who felt so inferior that she threatened to take her life; yet at the same

[1] New York: W. W. Norton and Co., 1950

time she insisted that she had reached full maturity as a person at the age of ten years! So be aware of what these self-effacing, martyr-like and "inferior" people are really doing. There is another side to them which you will soon learn. Sooner or later, in one way or another, they will demand a position superior to the rest of humanity. And that is nothing but pride. Let us call it by name.

Pride has to do with absurd pretensions about oneself or an "overhigh opinion of oneself" to quote the dictionary. The victim of pride leaves the reality which he really is and jumps into the realm of fantasy. There one can be whatever he wants to be – a medieval knight, superman, Napoleon, a ferocious lion, a timid mouse, a worm. But there is a price to pay, and that is nothing less than one's soul. We cannot be our true selves and the embodiment of our fantasy-idol at the same time. To the degree that we use our idols, to that degree we lose the identity God has given us.

The idol is always an outlandish conception of ourselves far beyond our means of attainment. Those who are in the grips of idolatry have a knack for carving out for themselves impossible goals. They go after an income they will never be able to earn; they expect their children to be perfect; they begin their college education when they should be thinking about retirement; they think of themselves as able to solve any problem, whip any opponent, hurdle any obstacle. Here we can see the key to this problem of inferiority. It is caused by preposterous goals which we have set for ourselves – goals which take no consideration of the actual abilities God has created in us. It seems to be one of God's laws that as the chosen goals in life exceed our capabilities, the sense of inferiority increases.

The secret of overcoming the subhuman feeling we get with an inferiority complex is something which Jesus Christ Himself gives to us in the Parable of the Talents. Each servant was given various amounts of money "to each according to his ability." The point of the parable is simply that we are to use what has been given us and stop comparing ourselves to others, because this is the road to an inferiority complex, if we are a one talent man. We are simply to live in reality. If you are a man with one talent, that is all the good Lord intended you to be and the Lord does not make mistakes. We can spend the rest of our lives fighting it and resisting the created fact, but it is both foolish and presumptuous to attempt to bend reality to our pet ideas. Reality simply does not give. It is wiser to accept ourselves for what we are, for in so doing we become real people. And only a genuine person can really know and enjoy God. One of our patients at the hospital stated it so well when he said, "It is hard to live with God and remain a phony."

It is, but we try, and in the attempt we become unstable and double-minded, as we will now see.

Chapter Sixteen
Double-mindedness

THE WORD DOUBLE-MINDEDNESS comes from James 1:8: "For that person must not suppose that a double-minded man, unstable in all his ways, will receive anything from the Lord." James was talking about wisdom. If a man wants it, "let him ask in faith, with no doubting."

Wisdom is not given to those who both believe and doubt at the same time. The mind must be single to find wisdom. A person must go in one direction rather than attempt the impossible feat of going in two opposite directions at the same time. It is difficult to find wisdom when we are single-minded. It is impossible when double-minded.

Sometime ago someone asked me, "What do you find to be the central problem with people?" That is not an easy question. I don't think I have the complete answer to it, but from the way it looks presently, a central problem is double-mindedness. Only I worded my reply a little differently to my friend. I said, "A basic problem with all of us is that we want the good things of life but refuse to pay the prices for them."

We want wisdom but we also want to retain our folly. We like the things of God but also cherish the pleasures of sin. We dearly "want to have our cake and eat it too" – that is, have our cake to eat even after we have eaten it!

Examples of this are not difficult to find. Think of Adam and Eve in the Garden of Eden where for some happy time they served and loved God. There was an intimate fellowship and love between them. I am sure it was in itself a beautiful and satisfying relationship. But Adam and Eve wanted more. They wanted to be like God. Undoubtedly theologians are correct when they tell us that the intention of our parents was rebellion against God, not merely the emulation of Him. It is not difficult already to perceive their double-mindedness. Adam and Eve loved and hated God simultaneously.

Now here is a curious fact about the spiritual life. People whose primary dedication of themselves is to God, do very well in life. People who live a predominantly godless life, though the ultimate satisfactions are not theirs, yet do tolerably well and are not terribly crippled by their conflicts. But the great mass of us poor souls who attempt to love and spurn God at the same time – we *suffer*. We place ourselves into excruciating conflicts when we try to give equal allegiance to the Truth and the Deceiver in the fantastically foolish hope that we can receive the benefits of *both*. In the end, we receive the benefits of *neither*. This is the tragic folly of double-mindedness.

Our Lord Jesus Christ was well aware of all this in His temptations. The temptations were gauged to test

Him for double-mindedness. Was Christ's allegiance only to His Father or would He do the bidding of Satan in order to secure bread to eat, kingdoms to rule, and to enjoy protection from danger? Upon whose "signals" would Christ act—the Father's or Satan's? Our Lord, as we know, successfully demonstrated His single-minded devotion to His Father.

Let us turn to a pastoral conversation which I had with a man who had an alcohol problem. This will illustrate the subtle ways double-mindedness enters into our lives.

PARISHIONER: Everyone has his troubles. I have mine. I went through the terrible experience of losing my wife. I don't know how to put it, to express the feeling. I was very lonely. I did not have the man in me, I could not face up to a problem. I started down hill, caring less and less. It got to a point where I could not go on.

PASTOR: You state it correctly, you could not face the problem. But I do not agree with you that you were not a man. You were and are a man.

PARISHIONER: But I could not face up to reality.

PASTOR: You were a man acting in a childish way but we must not lose sight of the fact that you are a man, a human person. What is bugging your life is patterns of behavior which are still childish. A child feels he cannot face up to the truth and solve a problem. He cannot, but grown people can. You are grown.

PARISHIONER: I *was* immature. I could not face up to the fact that I had lost two people dear to me in two months. Even my children went out of my life because my in-laws raised them after my wife died. I do not even know where my daughter lives. I do not want to ruin her home and live with her, though.

PASTOR: Of course not. They probably would want to see you, though, particularly if you are sober. They do not want you around with an alcohol problem.

PARISHIONER: I guess you are right. See, I left my children long ago, during the depression years. My in-laws raised them. I kept on working. I will tell you the truth—I was a gambler. Everybody did what he could to make a living in those days. I was a bookie.

PASTOR: So you chose an illegal operation.

PARISHIONER: I had to.

PASTOR: You chose to.

PARISHIONER *(after a thoughtful pause)*: I guess you are right.

The double-minded thinking occurs in the parishioner's desire to be a man but his refusal to live soberly; in the recognition of himself as a father but also his role as stranger to his children; in his desire to live both in the underworld and in a moral society. Inner conflict is inevitable on such a basis for life.

Paul Scherer tells of a man who was double-minded concerning Christ. " 'What would happen to me' said a man to his friend, 'if I tried to carry on my business as Christ would want me to do it? I'd be ruined!' 'And what will happen to you if you don't?' the other asked him quietly. 'What kind of ruin do you want?' "[1]

[1] Paul Scherer, *Love Is a Spendthrift* (New York: Harper and Row, 1961), p. 160. Used by permission.

This last question—"What kind of ruin do you want?"—is of great help to me when I am double-minded. Putting that kind of question to a problem seems to clarify the choice, though it does little to make the decision easier. But does not double-mindedness always boil down simply to a choice of "ruins," to use Scherer's word? There is always a price to pay (and a high price if what is desired is any good) for what we want. And, as if this were not enough, we inevitably choose against what we reject because every choice *for* something is always a choice *against* something else. For wise choices we pay a high price. Foolish choices cost us even more.

This means that we will inevitably suffer, whether for good or evil. We would dearly love to evade suffering but we cannot. Our Lord has built it into the very structure of life for "suffering produces endurance, and endurance produces character, and character produces hope" (Romans 5:3-4).

My pastor has more than once advised me to do two things with my suffering. The first is to make peace with it—stop resenting it. His second bit of counsel is even wiser. "Give yourself the right to suffer. Give up the claim that life must be easy."

I pass this good pastoral counsel on to you, knowing from my own experience, that it can help us steer clear of double standards and double-mindedness. God will give us single-mindedness, if only we are willing to suffer for it.

Chapter Seventeen
Idolized Guilt

I wish in this chapter to discuss the problem of guilt feelings in a person who is a Christian. You recognize here, I am sure, the double-mindedness problem we discussed in the last chapter for we are thinking now of a person who feels he is a Christian, yet one who is plagued by a sense of guiltiness.

Let us talk about a person who has already professed his faith in Jesus Christ, made a confession of his sins and sought the pardon of his Lord. Since these are sincere acts, there is no question about the response of pardon on the part of God. He welcomes the prodigal with open arms and there follows a joyous celebration in heaven. That is how *God* feels. But the feeling of reconciliation and pardon finds no place in the heart of this Christian. Intellectually he accepts the promises of God, but on the emotional level, he still feels guilty. Here is no assurance of pardon. Why?

To answer that question we must talk about one of the most troublesome problems of the human race — idolatry. By this I do not mean the false gods which gave the ancients so much trouble, nor even twentieth-century idols of money, sex and automobiles. The idols I refer to here are little images of *ourselves* which we treasure in the secret chambers of our minds. We have not really disposed of the troublesome problem of idolatry against which the Old Testament prophets continually railed; we have simply internalized the idols where the prophets of today cannot see them.

The most important thing to notice about an idol is that it is a fantasy representation of ourselves. Let us turn to an example of this and then conclude by showing the connection between idolatry and guilt feelings which may persist after forgiveness.

Adam Mudd is a student in a theological seminary. He came from a broken home. His father had an alcoholic problem which broke up the home when Adam was five years old. His mother worked and then remarried after about ten years. Though Adam was a good student, he always had deep misgivings about his ability. In college he did not feel any girl wanted to go on a date with him and for this reason he had little to do with girls. Actually, he was afraid of being rejected by them.

When I met Adam he was already in the seminary but rather anxious about his being there because he felt that the professors would discourage him in his calling if they really got to know him intimately. As a matter of fact, I knew the professors were glad to have him in seminary and they felt warmly about him as a person. Another student told me that Adam was an able student but he was unable to argue a point and if forced to do so, he would back down apologetically.

This is enough about Adam to allow us to see the fantasy idol of himself which he worships. The idol is a mental picture of himself as an inadequate, unlovable and failing person. The truth is that he is a good-looking, intelligent and sensitive human being with every reason to take his place in the human family. From a theological point of view, Adam is cherishing an idol as his model in life rather than aspiring to the fullness of the stature of Christ. Were he to really worship the living God, he would choose Christ as the goal and pattern of his life rather than the fantasy idol he carved out in the process of growing up.

Returning to the problem of guilt feelings which persist after the forgiveness of God has been granted, it is usually a cherished idol which causes all the trouble. How can a Christian *feel* like a Christian if he still inwardly sees himself as a sub-human, inferior and guilty person who has justifiably been stripped of a sense of worth and esteem? These are the very things which the new life in Christ gives us – a sense of dignity, a new and wonderful sense of being truly human, all that Paul means when he speaks of the new man in Christ. "Therefore, if any one is in Christ, he is a new creation; the old has passed away, behold, the new has come. All this is from God..." (II Corinthians 5:17,18). If our primary need is to prove that the idol of a guilty self is true, then though there may be intellectual assent to this verse, the joy of its truth will not hit us.

Thank God that our redeemed status before Him does not hinge on the degree to which we have assimilated the fact of pardon into our feelings! But

how needless the suffering over our past sins when the smile of God is upon us, when, just to prove the "worth" of *our* idol, we deny the fact of pardon by doubting that it is for us. It is a trick we have played on ourselves. To be sure it was not calculated or premeditated. Much of what we have described here is an unconscious process.

In the early years of childhood we form our idols without much awareness, but when we come to adulthood, it is time to put away the fantasies we have about ourselves and live in the real world which God has created. "...when I became a man, I gave up childish ways," says Paul (I Corinthians 13:11). Paul is perhaps the prime example of a person who could not rid himself of overwhelming guilt feelings until he gave up the idol of himself as one righteous through the Pharisaic law of men and substituted "the image of the likeness of Christ" in its place. This is what Paul meant when he said: "I through the law died to the law, that I might live to God. I have been crucified with Christ; it is no longer I who live, but Christ who lives in me..." (Galatians 2:19-20). Paul was completely identified with the ideas and goals of Christ — ideas and goals gotten through the power of Christ. Whatever Paul had was not of Paul but of Christ. Paul's identity was Christian rather than Pauline.

Perhaps you expect me to close this chapter and this section by offering suggestions on how to overcome the feeling of idolized guilt. I wish it were possible but it would be an exercise in folly. The most one can do is what I have done — simply clarify the issues and trust that the Spirit of God will solve these problems in His own way, at His own time. The more I deal with people in the grips of their idolatries, the more I understand that their destruction comes not when human might and power are applied against them, but when the problem is yielded to God for His solution.

If you suffer from idolized guilt, I suggest you wrap it up in a bundle, tie it tightly with the strings of your faith, and give it to God. He knows what to do with it. In another day, when I had many more answers than I now have, I thought this solution to the problem was evasive, even infantile. Since then, I have come to know God as the Problem-Solver of life.

Part IV
Coming to Maturity

Chapter Eighteen
Who Is a Normal Person?

IN OUR QUEST for a Christian identity, our goal is to attain "to mature manhood, to the measure of the stature of the fulness of Christ" (Ephesians 4:13). This is something quite different from "being normal" which is what so many people today have as their purpose in life. Let us address ourselves, for a moment, to this matter of normality.

Who is a normal person? The psychologists have lately come up with an attempt to answer this question and their spokesman is Dr. Marie Jahoda who wrote the book *Current Concepts of Positive Mental Health.*[1] She argues first, and I am sure we would all agree with her, that just because certain people find themselves in the middle of a statistical survey, does not make them normal in the sense of healthy. It makes them average and the average may be some very sick people. In a mental hospital ward, for example, most patients may hallucinate but the minority who do not are healthier. Dr. Jahoda prefers to speak of a normal person in the sense of a model

[1] New York: Basic Books, 1958.

person who meets a high standard of achievement. Such a person would have a "sense of selfhood," would realize his potentialities as a human being, would have a well-balanced personality, would be capable of independent action, would not distort reality, and would be able to "master the environment."

With full appreciation for the work of our psychological friends, I would like to outline the approach of a Christian pastor to this question before us.

First, I see Jesus Christ as the Norm. All measuring is to be done in terms of His perfect and full humanity rather than the constantly shifting average compiled from the masses, or even the human criteria set by psychological studies. We do not set our own standards for human health. The pattern is given to us in the words, deeds and person of Jesus Christ. When the questions, "What is a mature person?" and "Who is healthy?" are put to me, I answer: Jesus Christ is the epitome of maturity and health, and the details of all this are sufficiently revealed to us in the Scriptures.

But what does this mean specifically? Let us turn to an illustration at random from the life of our Lord.

Take, for example, His decision to die on the cross. The thing to observe about this decision is its source. It was the will of His Father and was fully agreed to by Christ. We might say that all the "signals" for this action came from the relationship between Christ and the Father. Jesus did not go to His disciples, His mother, His relatives or His friends to ask what He should do with his life, for then the "signals" would have come from without and Christ would have been the pawn of public opinion. Indeed, look at the entire life of Christ and you will find that He always received His directions from within. He never allowed Himself to be manipulated and He never marketed Himself to the person who would give Him the most in terms of affection and praise. He took His world into consideration (as with the Syro-Phoenician woman) but He always chose to act upon His world in terms of His values, rather than be acted upon by the values of people around Him. This, I submit, is maturity and health acted out for us in a Person.

The point we are making, however, is that we do not go to the statistical average in the human masses nor even to our good friends the psychologists to find the norm for our lives. We go to a quiet place where we can read the Bible and meet our Lord in prayer. You might even say we choose to be abnormal in this respect because we do not see the masses doing this too often. It has happened, however, that when a person emerges from this quiet place, he chooses a course of action which is decidedly abnormal in terms of society but is model behavior in God's sight.

I have a friend who did just that. He is a druggist in a large city which is notorious for its corrupt politicians. When the druggist opened his new store a few years ago, he applied for a city license and it was granted. A month after the award, an inspector came around and to the amazement of the druggist, the inspector found all kinds of violations—dirty shelves, old merchandise, poor records, etc. Now none of this was true, but nonetheless the license was in jeopardy. Next month the same thing happened and the month after that also, until finally a fellow-druggist gave my friend the message that five dollars each time to the inspector would clear the record.

This druggist is a Christian and you can see the dilemma into which he was cast. If he allowed himself to be coerced he would be denying his Christian values and become a participant to fraud – but he would stay in business. If he refused to pay bribe money, he would be continually harassed, possibly even lose his license. It was a tough spot to be in because he had to make a decision between being as "normal" as the majority of the druggists who paid the bribe and struggling to attain the values of the Norm, Jesus Christ.

He chose the Norm and thereby became socially abnormal. Providentially, he has not lost his license but he is continually harassed. That is the price he pays and he does not complain. This is what it costs to be Normal.

There are those who have criticized my friend for being a legalist. They tell him that he is doing this only because of a code of ethics which his conservative theology foists upon him rather than from his own internal values. He, however, affirms his subservience to the law of God and simply states that, in addition, to be coerced and defrauded is to be dehumanized and is a betrayal of one's true self. Even better, he makes no claim that people should approve or applaud his action – his signals are coming from within where the Norm resides.

Who is a normal person? Jesus Christ – and we, to the extent that we identify with Him.

Chapter Nineteen
Receiving a Gift Graciously

A MARK OF a mature Christian which I have come to prize highly is his ability to receive a gift. This is no small virtue for there are few people who really know how to receive a gift and even fewer who understand the nature of a gift. So let us look, first, at the nature of a gift.

A gift – if it is a true gift – is a freely-bestowed, unmerited favor. It is the embodiment of an attitude. The attitude is grace.

A gift, then, is something to which the beneficiary can lay no claim. If he can claim it, then he has a right to it and the element of grace is excluded.

These are elementary truths but they are often forgotten in the rush of daily activity. Even worse, we may spoil the good gifts we receive from God and fellow men by three unworthy, ungracious attitudes: the urge to pay for the gift; exaggerated concern over its cost; or the complaint that the gift is not enough. Let us look first at our urge to pay for the gift.

Often when we are given a gift, it is felt as an indignity, if not a downright insult to our persons. What is the reason for such a reaction? It is because we do not trust love. We feel it is too dangerous to be loved. Love always pleads that we return love, and we fear that this would coerce us. There is the fear, moreover, that a gift makes us inferior to the giver simply because we are on the receiving end. This damages our pride.

As we allow ourselves to be shaken by such fantasies, we look for ways in which to save face, to regain composure and communicate the impression of a splendid independence. One way of doing this is to offer to pay for the gift.

Perhaps we do not react this way too often with Christmas presents and birthday gifts, but thousands use this device on God. Said a friend of mine some time ago: "I can stand on my record. God knows I've tried to do my best. My reward is in store for me. If I had my life to live all over, I would have it the same."

Sometimes we seek to pay for gifts with gifts. I have known people to suffer greatly because they had received a gift and had no time to buy one in return for the donor. Or again, it is possible for a Christian to think of his peldge to the church as a return favor to God.

We never give up!

Let us look next at our exaggerated concern over the cost of a gift.

"You should not have done it!" is a familiar response to a gift. This is calculated to evoke even more "love" than is represented in the gift. You know what we are supposed to reply — "But I *wanted* to do it!" A side benefit to the beneficiary, of course, is that he sells himself as a humble, unworthy person. Recall the mock concern of Judas for the poor when Mary anointed our Lord's feet with expensive ointment.

This false concern is of a type with Christians who bemoan their unworthiness and insignificance *ad nauseam* in the face of God's blessings to them.

Preachers who are constantly impressing on their people "what it cost God to redeem us through His Son" are, I feel, ungracious beneficiaries. Continual, unrelenting cost-consciousness in the pastor's sermons serve no particular purpose except to create in the congregation a sense of guilt which is then used by the pastor to get his people to act in a certain way.

Finally, there is the complaint that the gift is not enough. How often do we complain to ourselves or our closest friends that some gift we have received is not good enough, or not expensive enough. Here is a part of a pastoral interview illustrating such an attitude toward God.

PASTOR *(speaking to a small group):* John is living on his memories. He lost his wife. He is resentful. He feels he should have had her longer than 38 years. It is not enough that God gave him 38 years with her. John had to have her 40 or 50 years at least.

JOHN: Is that wrong?

PASTOR: You judge yourself but consider that neither you nor I deserve our wives even for one year!

JOHN: Well, why do we get married then?

PASTOR: To love a wife God graciously gives us. But when He takes her away, it is ungrateful to bang our heads against a wall in a temper tantrum. John, do you think you and I have a *right* to our wives?

JOHN: Yes! In my retirement we could have lived together.

PASTOR: Yes, but I disagree with you on the right to have a wife. We don't even have a right to live. I can't say to God, "I have a right to be here today." Who in the world do I think I am? Do I tell the Almighty what rights I have, what He owes me, what I have coming? How many feet tall do I think I am?   (end of interview)

There is a better way.

One of the most difficult things in the world is to receive a gift graciously. That is, to receive it and really accept it with sincere gratitude to the benefactor for his love. Love — the very thing in life we want most — often frightens and angers us. When frightened, we evade love by offering to pay for the gift, thereby killing love with a commercial transaction. When angered, we attempt to castigate the donor either for his wastefulness or his stinginess.

Might not a better way be to make friends with the grace and love of persons? Accept such feelings and seek to do nothing but enjoyably feel them. Let the gift make a deep impression on your heart. Be an example to others of how to receive a gift graciously, for at another time you will want to be a loving donor.

And might your gift to another be the knowledge of Christ?

Chapter Twenty
The Secret of the
Overflowing Cup

THE PERSON identified with Christ is a thankful person. Thankfulness is a mark of his maturity. The attitude of gratitude, however, is not easy to come by. I believe that possibly the most difficult phrase in the Bible to say and *mean* is the sentence, "My cup runneth over." Deep down in our hearts, most of us believe we hold in our hands a half-full cup.

Sometime ago I did some work among the men and women on the "skid row" in Trenton, New Jersey. I found it to be a street of discontented, broken people. There was a question I often put to them which brought out this feeling of discontent.

"Could you be satisfied," I would ask, "with an offer of three square meals, a bed in which to sleep, a cup of hot coffee and a good friend with whom to talk? Would you square off for that?" I could offer this because I was associated with the Salvation Army in Trenton. Would you believe it, not once did I get an affirmative answer. They all wanted more, much more.

These people are an example of our incessant claims upon ourselves, our world and God. We need a job better than the one we possess. The wife is not as attractive as her husband would like her to be. The children are not geniuses. The dog is not of the right pedigree. The bank balance is too low. The church to which we belong is too dead. Young people today are not what they should be. Our money is not worth what it used to be. The wife spends too much time gardening. The husband is not affectionate enough. The children take everything for granted.

Perhaps all of these things are true but we should still ask: How much do we need to fill our cups? They often have no bottom.

Last evening a couple came to my study and on the way over, narrowly escaped having a fatal accident. A large truck swung into the path of their car within inches of them. When my friends arrived at my study they were trembling. They had come to talk about their marital problems but somehow we never got around to talking about them, though I knew that they were by no means small problems. They had suddenly diminished to a point where the joy of being alive was a fact of far more importance and interest to them. They simply sat in their chairs and said, "Just think! We could be in the hospital or the grave by now. It is good to be in one piece. It is a pleasure just to breathe, to be alive." They were satisfied and at peace with what they had.

As long as there is any craving, the cup has no bottom. Because of this interesting fact, I have long been a student of the great Meister Eckhart[1] and his concept of disinterest.

Disinterest is the practice of nonattachment to everything which is creaturely. In one of his sermons, Eckhart says: "Perfectly disinterested, a man has no regard for anything, no inclination to be above this or below that, no desire to be over or under; he remains what he is.... He desires only to be one and the same; for to want to be this or that is to want something; and the disinterested person wants nothing.... Know then, that a mind unmoved by any contingent affection or sorrow, or honor, or slander, or vice, is really disinterested — like a broad mountain that is not shaken by a gentle wind."

The disinterested person is not at all one who is uninterested in life. Nor is he detached from life. The person of which Eckhart speaks is in the middle of life, and he tastes and enjoys life whenever he can. He affirms life but never idolizes it, nor does he allow his affections to be captured by it. He is a true pilgrim who has chosen to truly relinquish his claims upon temporal things because he has fully invested himself in God.

May I say, parenthetically, that I cannot understand why the modern clergyman reverently draws so much of his water from the wells of psychiatry and psychology when there is so much pure and tested water in the cisterns of the Christian church. Do we

[1] Meister Johannes Eckhart was a Christian mystic who lived early in the 13th century. The quotations which follow are from the translation by Raymond Blakney, Harper and Row, 1941, and are used by permission.

ministers long for effective, proven pastoral approaches which will really help our people with their deepest problems? We have one right before us. Let us learn what Eckhart discovered long ago about disinterest.

The road to peace of mind and soul is through disinterest. It is impossible to find rest for our souls if we allow our insatiable desires to dictate a never-ending list of wants. As God sees us, He must often be reminded of little children who enjoy looking through the Sears, Roebuck catalog. As they page through it they sigh: "I'd like *that.* I *need* it." Our desires often turn into demanding claims that we *must* have this or that. Indeed, we will not be happy or contented until it is our possession! How different the disinterested person, "who wants nothing, and neither has he anything of which he would be rid! (He) has no prayer, for to pray is to want something from God. He prays only to be uniform with God."

Disinterest makes room for God, for "to be full of things is to be empty of God while to be empty of things is to be full of God."

This is Eckhart's application of the God vs. mammon teaching of our Lord. Then he goes on to say that "disinterest brings knowledge of God; cut off from the creature, the soul unites with God."

Come, be a Christian mystic and you will then know this secret of true mental and spiritual health: *God is our only true treasure.*

The test of this truth in our lives is made by the willingness to part with any "thing" in our environment. We are not really ready to own a house or a new car until we could, if need be, live without resentment were these taken from us. The same is true of our work, our jobs. We are unfit for the work in which we are engaged unless we can give it up to God should He ask it of us, and do it without bitterness or malice either toward God, our employer or ourselves.

But we can give up this "treasure" only if we are fully invested in God.

And so a poor man, an unemployed man, a person burdened with many cares and worries – such people need not come to God pretending that their cups are half-full. Our cups overflow so long as we are filled with God, though we be stripped of all else.

Contemplate and enjoy God and we will find that what we hold in our hands looks more like a spouting geyser than an overfilled cup.

Chapter Twenty-One
The Treasure
of a Mystical Experience

THOSE WHO are truly enthralled by Christ, I have noticed, seem to have a wonderful, trustful appreciation for the ineffable mysteries of life. I have noticed this particularly with Christians who have had ecstatic, mystical experiences. The weak in Christ may discount the value of such religious experiences, but those who are established in Him prize them greatly. Let us look at a few examples.

A man with a severe depression was dozing under a tree. His mind was somewhat confused and anxious but not so much that a drowsiness could not overtake him. In this state of half-wakefulness a wonderful experience occurred. He felt the palm of a hand move soothingly over his forehead and a kind voice said: "You have nothing to fear because I will help you to survive it all." An indescribable feeling of peace and joy followed. This gentleman regards this experience as a vision from God and a sure promise from the Almighty that victory will crown his life.

A wonderful Christian couple in their late seventies were both fighting off an attack of the flu. The husband slept on the davenport so as not to disturb his wife in the adjoining bedroom. The door was half-open but neither one could see the other. The husband awoke in the middle of the night and saw a blinding light.

The old gentleman was surprised with his own reaction to the dazzling brightness for rather than panicking, he was enchanted by it as he sat on his couch. But now came the climax. Emerging from the brightness was a man with his arms outstretched in blessing. The old man was transfixed and following this he experienced a wonderful period of peace and rest in which every ache and pain disappeared from his body. After about half an hour he went to tell his wife what had happened and was startled to find her standing by the bed. It was difficult for her to contain her joy as she said, "I know, John, I saw Him too." Both of them have no doubt but that it was a vision of Christ which they saw simultaneously.

One more example but of a different kind. A man in the middle years had always been terrified by the thought of his death. At this particular time he was under much strain because of family problems but this did not deter him from going to church Sunday morning. He arrived early and sat quietly in the pew while the organist played a Bach prelude. Suddenly the sun broke through the clouds and the church window permitted a breath-taking view of the landscape. At this moment the man had an overwhelming feeling of ecstasy which lasted about a minute. This feeling was terminated by a thought which entered his mind with great force and conviction; he was ready to die. Right here in the church he was ready to die, because of what he described as a "deep feeling of completion within." From that moment, he was never again terrorized by the thought of death.

I have talked much with each of the people who have had these visions and learned a great deal from them.

One reaction which each person shared was the feeling that they had experienced something of inestimable value which was theirs alone! Almost as if to say: "This is *my* vision and I make no claim that it makes sense to you. No one need believe it and no one can take it from me but I know. I know."

There was also in each case a stress situation which preceded the vision – depression, the flu, family trouble. This seems to be the precondition of a vision – that we *need* it because of a crisis in our lives. A study of the great mystics reveals that it was often after "fasting and praying" for long periods in which the body and mind were severely taxed, that they were ready for mystical communion.

As for a scientific explanation of these visions, frankly, I am not too interested. For one thing, visions in the hands of the psychologists (with the exception of William James) have not been given a sensitive and understanding treatment. The insinuation is often made that people who experience visions are probably hallucinating. And since hallucinations are one evidence of psychosis, such people are sick or at best, abnormal. Others feel that a religious vision is a regression into the earliest childhood fantasies of omnipotence and the strong urge to be protected and cared for by a parent. The source of the experience, we are told, is to be found prior to the second year of human development because only such a preverval period would explain the ineffable character of the vision. Very learned – and useless! I have lost interest in having visions explained psychologically because the explanations I have read usually empty the experience of a sense of wonder and meaning which is so basic to true religion.

With any religious phenomenon, it is important to ask meaningful questions about it. It is so easy and unprofitable to ask, "How does the vision work? What caused it? Is it real? How can we explain it?" These questions are symptomatic of the illness of our culture for they are the product of detached, depersonalized people who spend their days as spectators of the world rather than participants in it. Such a person comes away from a great play saying: "It was a skillful performance." It never occurs to him to say, "I *liked* it," or possibly decide to become an actor.

A proper question to ask, it seems to me, is "What does the vision *mean* to the person having it?" Does he draw great inspiration from it? As a result, has he made some decisions or adopted a new course of action? And are these in line with the principles of the kingdom of God? If so, the vision has done a priceless service and praise God for it. There is no need to analyze it. Enjoy it and Him who gave it to you.

Part V
A Christian Identity
in Marriage

Chapter Twenty-Two
A Christian Identity
in the Home

THE THRESHOLD under your front door is more than a piece of oak installed to keep the windy drafts outside. It is a divider between two worlds.

The outside is where most of us function best. We are nice to the customers who come into our business establishments. We visit good friends with whom it is pleasant to drink coffee. Even our relatives are, for the most part, nice to drop in on. In a word, the world outside our thresholds is such that we really function quite well as followers of Christ.

Something strange often happens to many of us, however, when we step across our thresholds into our homes and join in that communal activity we call family life. We feel almost as though we become completely different persons. Many of us are baffled by the alarming contrast between our rather pleasing conduct outside the threshold and our cantankerousness on the inside.

A fellow pastor came to me with this very problem a few days ago. This man has charge of a parish whose greatest distinction is that it consistently offers each of its pastors the option either of leaving or staying and going mad. The present man, however, though he has gone through deep waters with his people, is staying with them. He truly has a pastor's heart. His love for his unruly parishioners is wonderful to see. When someone blasts him with anger, he accepts the dubious gift and tries to understand. Some time ago a hostile female parishioner took one of the pastor's books and began hitting him on the head with it. This good man turned his cheek in forgiving silence, although it is true he wondered out loud with me whether his reaction was prompted by a state of grace or a state of shock. I felt the former because this man consistently does an outstanding piece of work in his church.

What brought the pastor to my study asking for help? His family life. It presented problems with which he could not cope. It seemed that the moment he crossed the threshold of his home to be with his family, a different feeling came over him. Gone was all the patience and understanding he had used with his parishioners but an hour ago. If supper was a little late, the mistress of the manse was set up as a target for a few hostile barbs. Her husband was altogether different at home than at work. In the parish, the pastor's love for the children of the Sunday school knew no end, but at home, his own children had to put up with a very touchy, grouchy father. It was easy to love his congregants, but why did he become downright nasty so often with those who, deep down, he loved even more than his congregation? The contradiction between the pastor and the father was causing such anxiety in this man that he was driven to seek help, fearing that he was some kind of dual personality. I disagreed with his diagnosis but not with the fact that he was saddled with some heavy problems.

Most parents experience something of this conflict between a disrupted, even painful home life and an astonishingly smooth life outside of the home. The reason for this has something to do with the closeness of the relationship. In the intimacy of family life, the feelings, both positive and negative, become more intense. There is an increased risk not only of hurting but of being hurt. Our positive feelings bless us with lasting and deep satisfactions but the negative ones can burn a hellish hole in our exposed egos.

Every family, whether it wishes to or not, presents each of its members with an invitation to closeness. Our closest human relationships are between husband and wife; between parents and children. Because of the intensity of this intimacy, however, more can go wrong and more destruction can be wrought in family life than in any other sphere of human activity. On the other hand, our families are also the means into some of life's deepest satisfactions.

It is the thesis of this book that the deepest and best satisfactions in life can be had only as God forms a Christian identity in us. We get into no end of trouble when we try to live life according to the pattern of the models produced by our prideful fantasies. Our model is Christ. Christ formed in us—which is exactly what it means to have a Christian identity.

But why steer the course of this book at this point into a discussion of the family? For three reasons.

First, the formation of a Christian identity cannot really take place in any other place than the home. This is obviously true for the children (and so we will talk about raising children), but it is also true for husbands and wives. One of the very good reasons God established the institution of marriage was so that people in it could grow up.

The family is the culture in which the growth (or lack of growth) of persons takes place. Family life is, at once, the most difficult setting in which this can take place and yet, the most fertile. If, by the mercies of God, growth as a Christian person takes place in the family, we may be fairly well assured that the person will exhibit Christian maturity in the other areas of human life. The family, therefore, is the crucial factor in the formation of a Christian identity. There is a second reason why we now turn to a consideration of the Christian family. We must think more concretely, using specific examples and life-situations. It is easy to talk on and on as we search for a Christian identity but far more will be accomplished by looking closely at the intimate realities of our home life.

And not least, we turn now to a study of marriage and child rearing because we wish to be thoroughly Christian in our approach to these tasks. I do not hesitate to speak of marriage and child rearing as tasks. If a marriage succeeds and a child turns out well, it is because good work has been done by the parents, God working through them. In the same way, if a family is to be a Christian family, it will be because Christ is formed in us (Galatians 4:19). Such families do not just happen. They are formed by the things that we do or do not do.

Let us now turn to the practical problems of marriage and after that, the problems of raising children.

Chapter Twenty-Three
Parent-Child Marriages

THERE IS A REASON why an engine stalls, a heart stops beating, or a mind becomes ill – perhaps many reasons. There are also reasons why marriages run dead and sometimes disintegrate. This chapter is the first of several dealing with the causes of marital problems, one of which may be seen in the mother-son marriage.

This marriage is a painful situation in which the husband defaults in the use of an authority which he is supposed to have and use. He simply declines to make decisions or to take any initiative unless, of course, he is compelled to do so either by his wife or a particular situation. In such tasks as disciplining the children, writing checks and paying bills, making decisions about where to live and what to do – such a husband feels he just cannot make up his mind about these things.

Into this authority-vacuum rushes a concerned wife who feels she must rescue her weak husband by grabbing the part he should be playing, if the marriage is to continue with any success at all. She feels she has no alternative other than to wear her husband's pants over her skirts. This is a feat which makes it most difficult, to say the least, for her to have any genuine feminine appeal.

Whether we say that a wife "acts like a mother toward her husband" or that she "wears the pants in the family," it means in either case that the wife wields authority over her husband. The decision-making machinery is taken over by her and frequently she begins to enjoy her new task in a perverted sort of way. It is she, now, who decides where vacations are to be spent, how the family budget money is to be used, what duties the children are to perform and how much spending money her husband is to hold in his hand – in his hand, I say, because he is without pockets, having given his pants away.

True, we joke about this kind of marriage but in all seriousness, it is a most painful situation for the people involved. Each inflicts gross indignities upon the other. Both parties feel humiliated and guilty and understandably so, since they are making choices which are in violation of the way God set up marriages to work. Such marriages violate His laws – laws which He ordained to protect and help us.

I realize that this analysis of the mother-son marriage makes rather depressing reading, but before I become more positive, I would ask your patience in looking at another kind of parent-child marriage which we call the father-daughter marriage.

"You are nothing but a dictator!" shouts the daughter-like wife to her husband. "You and Hitler belong together!"

The wife is right. There is a kind of "marriage" in which a wife defaults in the use of an authority God intended her to have. The husband rushes in to rescue the marriage by taking complete control of the womanly tasks.

I know of a man who, soon after marriage, sent his wife out of the kitchen because he knew more about cooking than she did. He was not satisfied with the way she was doing it, so *he* took over. That same man would never allow his wife or children to buy clothes unless he was in the store to approve the purchases. Even worse, he actually selected the clothes he wished his wife to wear! I know this is an extreme case but it is the true story of a well-educated, well-heeled man.

There is something more I must tell you about this man and his wife. Their marriage began in a father-daughter pattern but after about five years of that, they both became so sick of it that one day the husband announced: "I've had it. From now on you can have charge of the whole family. *You* worry about us from now on."

And would you believe it—from that day, the marriage swung into a mother-son orbit. When finally the husband arrived at my study he was complaining that he felt "like the fifth and last child in the family."

My point here is that the same couple can fluctuate between these two types of marriage. But there is something even more important to notice and it is that the relationship *can* change. That means there is hope. Hope materialized in this particular marriage, for in about the twentieth year of marriage they are finally learning to live as husband and wife!

So there is hope but also a few things to do.

First, face the truth about your marriage. It may be that you have been deluding yourself for many years into thinking that you were a very happy and compatible couple. Stop living a lie. Your education, money and prestige makes no difference. Only complete honesty and the courage to face facts are what we need if we really mean business in altering our marriages.

Second, it is extremely doubtful that you can alter the course of your marriage without the help of a third party. Without such help there is a real danger you will blow the marriage apart. I suggest you turn to your pastor. I think my reasons for such advise are sound. Your pastor is not only trained to understand how a healthy, Christian marriage really works, but he *believes* in it himself! Moreover, he will help both of you to submit to the living Christ in the settlement of your problems. The way out is by husband and wife surrendering *not* to each other (that comes later) but to Christ. This is what we mean by a Christ-centered marriage. Without Christ in the picture, a real resolution of conflict is doubtful, because who can submit to an equal without resentment? And even if one does, *why* should he? Christ is *the* Reconciler. Your pastor represents Him and will help you live in Christian marriage.

Finally, a basic rule to remember is that the only changes you have a right to claim are changes which you, with God's help, make in yourself. The temptation is to insist that your partner's behavior be altered before you make any changes. Such a course will kill the marriage. Husbands! if you really feel that "it's a woman's world" and your wife treats you like a son, the thing for you to do is simply begin slowly and lovingly to play the part of the husband. Leave both your wife and the changes she should make in God's hands. It would take longer than a lifetime to convince your wife that she should change. Nor should she take the initiative. If you take the initiative, two people are in position to change, while if she changes first, you will remain unchanged and immature as you have always been. The Lord spare you from that! So I urge you with Paul to quit yourself like a man before you go to your grave without ever having lived through the issues of your life.

Now, that's tough and hard! I know. But life was never intended to be a party. It's a school, and all of us attend it.

Chapter Twenty-Four
The Authoritarian Mind
in Marriage

MY PURPOSE during the next few minutes is to say something which will assist us in receiving more of the "mind of Christ." God be thanked for the progress He has already made in us. We are not where we were. In this chapter I wish to briefly explain a pitfall which may severely retard our growth in grace. It happens when we assume an authoritarian mind—to the damage of the mind of Christ in us.

The authoritarian mind is the mind of a dictator. Out of this mind come commands and orders, threats and tongue-lashings, manipulation of people, disregard for persons, and anger. The human mind, in fantasy about itself, pretends to possess a super-human omniscience which always knows what is best for the mass of dull, ordinary human beings.

The authoritarian mind lives by legalisms. This loveless "law" is imposed upon lazy people who have chosen to be obedient to the authoritarian mind in return for its care and protection. Without these "deals" there would be no such mind.

The authoritarian mind looks very powerful. There is no question about its ability to destroy, but it has no power to do good, nor to truly love.

This mind of which we are speaking is a master in whipping people into line to do what it wants. The major device used is guilt. Just make the underling feel a little guilt in breaking the code of the lawgiver, and he will jump right back into line.

The reason for this is to be found in that the underling has projected his powers into the authoritarian person. This makes the slave feel subhuman. Such people feel they need to be cared for or else they will die. Who will take care of them if not this eleven-foot tall authoritarian savior? What he says must be done, or else those under him will feel very guilty about destroying themselves and offending the very hand which feeds them.

Before we turn to an example of authoritarianism, let me point out that the legalisms which it imposes on people are poles apart from valid laws. Such laws are for the order of society unto the good of people and the glory of God. Legalisms on the other hand, dehumanize and thereby destroy people, dishonor God, and feed the diabolic fantasies of the authoritarian legalist.

And while we are making distinctions, let us also make one between authority and authoritarianism. Authority we need. It makes a valid use of power and intends our good. It keeps order and permits us to live. Authoritarianism is a humorless caricature of authority and even worse, exploits us.

The opposite of authoritarianism is equalitarianism—a concept which, I believe, finds its roots squarely in the Scriptures, as I will point out later. But first, an example in marriage.

After a beautiful courtship John and Mary were married, but in a short time John began to act differently toward his wife. For example, he had formerly been very generous with money but now he put Mary on a very strict food-budget. When she asked about his earnings, he was evasive and even accused her of mistrusting him. When they would go on a trip, Mary would sometimes suggest a good route to travel but she has since given this up because John simply exploded at her and obstinately set out on his own route.

John always had strong, rigid opinions. One of them was that all people should eat slowly and thoroughly chew their food. He himself was a very slow eater and always insisted that his children never finish before him. If they emptied their plates before him, he treated this as disobedience and became angry. When Mary later interceded a bit for the children, he became furious and told her that as far as he was concerned, she too was a child!

Mary was hurt by all this, but she knuckled under, not once, but every time. It seemed the only way to live with a man like John. The longer she lived with him, however, the more she resented him. She loved him but it was difficult to feel the love because it was burdened with fear; she also hated him but she felt impotent to assert herself because, for the sake of the children, the marriage had to be held together.

Maybe John was right, thought Mary. Perhaps she was just a child living with her children. And John was their father. But who, then, was her husband? It was becoming apparent that her marriage was falling apart and she felt panic-stricken but helpless.

What we are dealing with here is the problem of the self-effacing person. I feel Mary is making a terrible mistake. She is swiftly being transformed into a doormat with the consequent loss of all human dignity and Christian self-respect.

It is true that Mary has always justified her actions with such words as "forgiveness," "humility," and "turning the other cheek." But there are two things which betray her posture as basically unchristian.

The first is that she is *always* backing down and "eating dirt," as she puts it. She does this not as an occasionally well-chosen act but as a consistent way of life. With our Lord, His humility and turning of the other cheek was a well-chosen, selected act—else He could never have exposed the Pharisees and given the money-changers in the temple the feel of his whip twice over.

In certain situations Jesus asserted Himself. In others, He was the "lamb that is led to the slaughter." On what basis did He choose His behavior?

This is a question which I am still studying, but I will share with you what I have found so far. It seems that it has most to do with whether or not Christ was being "set up." When His enemies set Him up to retaliate, resist, return anger for anger and hatred for hatred, our Lord refused to play along. He turned the cheek. He refused to become angry just because they were angry, to return blow for blow. Christ would not allow His behavior to be determined on the basis of what other people were doing to Him.

Whatever He did was done because of His inner values and choices, not someone's else's. Out of His inner values He spoke out against issues on which *He* chose to express Himself.

Returning to Mary in our illustration, we can now see the second reason why she should change her behavior toward John. Authoritarian John is always setting her up for self-effacement and Mary is meekly cueing into John's problem. Such behavior is the kiss of death for their marriage, for Mary is acting as she is, not out of strength but out of weakness. She is making a deal with the devil—peace at any price. It would be far better if Mary would strike out for an equalitarian relationship.

God did not intend that husbands "play god" to their wives, nor vice versa. God did not set up a master-race and a slave-race of people. We are all people, "created equal" as the Constitution (the world's most equalitarian document except for the Bible) puts it. People differ as to *function*, which is something they should freely choose; as to *office* which others freely bestow upon selected individuals; as to *talents* which God bestows on some. But we are all equal in worth and dignity through Christ who knows us neither as slave or free, nor as male or female (Galatians 2).

I think Mary should press for an equal relationship with her husband. This will mean much struggle and pain, both for her and for John. But if by God's grace and love she can effect some changes in herself, John will also begin to change, for dictators go out of business when they find themselves without pawns to push around.

If Mary, then, will truly act as a new person, showing neither fear nor anger but love for John, he will soon feel the "burning coals upon his head"

(Romans 12:20). A man, even an authoritarian man, can stand only so much of that.

Mary should not allow herself to be overcome by John's evil outlook; nor should she be overcome by the evil of self-destruction within herself. In this double sense, the advice of Paul is true: "Do not be overcome by evil, but overcome evil with good" (Romans 12:21).

Chapter Twenty-Five
Sex

SEX – that much discussed subject – may play a part in the breakdown of marriage. But I am not one of those who believe that all marital problems begin with sexual trouble. The fact is, in most cases the sexual relationship is usually the last thing to break down. Yet, it is an important factor particularly when a marriage deteriorates to a point where it becomes a brother-sister relationship.

This is the tragic, painful situation when husband and wife no longer have sexual relations. I call this a brother-sister marriage because of the strong social taboo against sexual relations with one's brother or sister. We call that incest.

Would you believe it – a husband and wife, who on the honeymoon felt warm electricity when they touched each other, can let the marriage fall apart to the point where they will actually feel pain by the touch of the marriage partner? This is a tragedy, to say the least. The very thought of sexual intercourse becomes a repugnant idea in such a marriage. And though that is bad enough, something even more terrifying comes to mind. Each party begins to ask questions like, "What is wrong with me? Am I dying sexually? Am I falling apart? If sexual desire leaves me, does it ever return?" Talk about *suffering!*

How did such a situation ever come about?

Largely because of resentments. A very important point to learn about resentments is that such feelings accumulate, layer upon layer so to speak, and eventually form a barrier which walls off the person from his partner. A few of these resentments might be justifiable and if this is the case, one should take action, even drastic action, to arouse and correct the marriage partner. The vast majority of our resentments, however, are without foundation. They are productions from our inner, fantasy world.

I recall one such man who complained to me that he was angry with his wife for shopping at an expensive market. This family was loaded with money but, nonetheless, the husband would grind his teeth as his wife took off for that market each Saturday. There was something else about his wife he could not stand. She made too much noise when she chewed celery. They entertained guests often and this husband had all he could do to contain himself when the celery dish came to his wife. By this time he was saying to himself: "Will that thick-headed wife of mine never learn that she embarrasses us all by eating celery?" The market and celery were only two of a long list of his resentments against his wife.

In such an emotional atmosphere, sexual feeling gradually fades away.

At the other end of the scale are what we can call playboy-bunny marriages. Here sex is glorified. It is everything to both parties, which is to say that there is little else in the marriage that draws them together.

It is not at all unusual for two such people to have an extremely active sexual life and yet really despise each other. Think of the promiscuous Don Juan and his prostitutes. I am thinking now, however, of a happier kind of marriage, yet one in which sex is the main attraction.

One of the worst things that can happen to such a marriage is for the wife to become pregnant. For one thing, it throws her all out of shape. For another, the period of a month before and after the birth of the child imposes an intolerable restriction upon sexual activity in the marriage—where there must be no interference!

Many Hollywood marriages are of this type. More examples are found among people who marry in their mid-teens. I do not say that this kind of marriage is the most common type, but there are enough around to warrant talking about them.

The current sexual revolution, you know, encourages this trend. Our culture boldly proclaims the message that the ultimate pleasures in life are sexual. This premise is accompanied by the quiet assumption that everyone has an absolute right to his pleasure by any means. It is followed by a determined, crusading resolution to break down all barriers which Christianity has erected to preserve a proper place for sexuality. But *Time* magazine is right in saying: "When sex is pursued only for pleasure, or only for gain, or even only to fill a void in society or in the soul, it becomes elusive, impersonal, ultimately disappointing."

Let us try to understand the function of sexuality.

From a Christian point of view, it is crucial to understand that we are not first of all male or female. We are *people, God's* people, who have sexuality but are not ultimately male or female. This is made clear to Christians in Paul's statement that "there is neither male nor female; for you are all one in Christ Jesus." In other words, sex is secondary; our identity as persons in Christ is primary. I am a Christian person before I am a male.

God ordained that the human spirit (I prefer this term to *person)* would be expressed and strengthened through his sexuality. Here I speak of the very deepest purpose of sexuality. It is to express the love of one spirit for another. It is also to be strengthened by the union of these two spirits.

The climax of sexual experience is the nearly total elimination of spiritual loneliness. It is that sacred moment when spirits who really care for each other join. This comes to expression physically, but really, body and spirit can never be separated. The total person is involved in union in marriage. The two become one flesh, as Scripture puts it.

If we really believe that the total person is involved—that one should give his "all" in marriage—it follows that there will be nothing to give to a third party. On the basis of this simple bit of reality, God ordains that we should lead chaste lives before marriage, and upon entering it be faithful and true to the beloved.

Great fulfillment in sexual relationships is experienced by people who understand and affirm the spiritual dimension of sex. Since God make us all human spirits, all people may know something of the lasting joys of the spiritual realm. Yet unless husband and wife find place in their marriage for the divine Spirit as the Source of strength, the bond of faithfulness and the higher object of their affections, there is great danger that their sexual life will either die or turn into animal lust, examples of which clutter our culture.

Chapter Twenty-Six
Sexual Relationships
Outside of Marriage

I AM ASSUMING that you, as a Christian, wish to submit to the lordship of Christ. Our Lord has spoken on the matter of sexual conduct. We are to be chaste before marriage and faithful within it. The God who created us as sexual beings has spoken. That is enough. Christians submit to His authority.

But immediately a great cry goes up throughout the earth. A complaining world shouts this accusation at God: You are arbitrary!

Now I dislike it when people feel that they have to defend God, so I will try to avoid this. But it seems to me entirely appropriate to point out that all God's laws have solid reasons behind them. None of the commandments are arbitrary. The Christian church should speak of the reasons behind God's laws, not to fortify the authority of the Almighty but rather that we may praise His kind wisdom and concern for us.

The Seventh Commandment, "Thou shalt not commit adultery," was given for good reasons. Terrible damage is caused to *us* through violation of this law. I wish to point out just three ways in which sexual relationships outside of marriage damage the people involved.

There is the damage caused by living in a world of fantasy and falsehood. Ultimately, we have only two choices. Either we live in the real world, the world of truth, or we live in the world of delusions and lies. There is a straight line between them. A close study of the life of Jesus shows that He consistently sided with the truth, with reality. It is perhaps the most basic principle in the kingdom of God.

Sex outside of marriage—either pre-marital or extramarital—is "play marriage" which is no marriage. It is a situation in which two people pretend to be married. The basis of the relationship is falsehood, a lie, a delusion.

Is that a serious matter? Or perhaps we should ask, is it damaging to me as a person? The answer is surely *yes*, very much so. We know that to be true from a study of mental illness. The problem of the mentally ill person invariably boils down to a disturbance in his relationship to reality. A person with an anxiety neurosis may be terrified by countless fears, none of which have a basis in the real world. One of my psychotic parishioners feels absolutely certain that he really does not possess a human body and no amount of evidence to the contrary has yet dislodged his fantasy. The homosexual is in fantasy concerning the sexual identity of himself and others. The alcoholic is in fantasy about how to solve his life-problems.

One could go on to illustrate the unending tragedy and misery caused by a capitulation to the world of falsehood. The world of falsehood is very closely related to the world of insanity. Hence the seriousness of a capitulation to such a world. This happens, I feel, when one pretends to be married to one who is not his wife or husband.

There is secondly, the damage caused by guilt. There is a law written indelibly in the heart of man and, in the case of many, reinforced by the revealed Word, which is transgressed when one is sexually promiscuous. All people have this law and all feel guilty when it is violated. I say "all" people, but I must qualify that by saying that individuals and groups who have so violated their consciences to a point where they no longer work—which it is possible to do—would, I agree, feel no guilt.

Morally sensitive people do feel guilt when they violate the laws of marriage. Indeed, they *should* feel guilty if they have any character at all, as O. Hobart Mowrer points out.

This guilt is always diabolically destructive to the person carrying it, for it has the effect of fracturing his entire moral code. We cannot break a little piece of law. Once this process of breaking the moral code begins, it may lead to the fragmentation of the entire personality.

King David is an example to us of moral fracturing. While Uriah, a soldier in David's army, was waging war, King David had sexual intercourse with Bathsheba, Uriah's wife, and she became pregnant. David quickly summoned Uriah from the battlefield and told him to spend the night at home with his wife, hoping thereby to bury the question of the child's paternity. But Uriah the Hittite had his moral house in order and would not sleep with his wife while his men were in battle.

The next night David succeeded in getting Uriah drunk but still he would not sleep with his wife. The king, now thoroughly demoralized, ordered Uriah to be placed in battle where, upon the withdrawal of supporting troops, he would be sure to be killed. He was. David married Bathsheba.

The moral fracture continued to a point of total moral blindness where David could not recognize himself in a little parable which Nathan the prophet told him. In the parable Nathan exposed him completely, after which David made a sincere confession, but that did not turn aside the severe penalties on him.

We see here the action of sin and guilt, particularly how they reinforce and perpetuate each other until one's moral house is a shambles.

I think it is always so in varying degrees with sexual relations outside of marriage.

Consider, finally, the damage caused by an unspiritual union. Marriage was intended by God to be a spiritual union of a man and a woman into "one flesh" (Ephesians 5).

Curiously, most civilized people accept this, for no one today seriously argues for polygamy or polyandry. Most people just seem to accept monogamy as right. I am not exactly sure why they do this but could it be that people know deep down that marriage should be a spiritual union and that this union cannot flourish if competitive third parties endanger the relationship. If a person chooses to know many persons of the opposite sex in the sacred intimacy of sexual intercourse, he can only give an insulting fraction of himself to his "beloved." There can be no genuine union of spirits in such a marriage because the gift of one's self is always partial. The act of sexual intercourse then becomes an animal gesture and a biological act without the exalted unity of spirits which it was meant to express. In Christian marriage, God discloses to us the mystery of Christ and His church as two spirits are truly made on in the mystery of the sexual act.

I feel strongly that the current attitudes toward sex and marriage coming to expression in the so-called "sexual revolution" reflect the moral disintegration of our society. Established Christian standards of conduct are under attack because a "new morality" is needed for today, we are told.

This is a lie.

The "new morality" cry is a cover-up for people who wish to destroy Christian ethics simply because it costs more than they care to pay and because they are willing to settle for a cheap marriage.

We get what we pay for. Cheap price, cheap goods. Whatsoever a man soweth, that shall he also reap.

Chapter Twenty-Seven
Christ-Centered Marriage

THE BASIC PROBLEM of marital discord in many cases is simply that the relationship was never set up right in the first place. No marriage is set up to function as the Designer and Creator intended it to function unless Jesus Christ stands in the center of the relationship.

What do we mean by a Christ-centered marriage? To speak of a Christ-centered marriage is not a cliché. It is *the* key to marriage. Without it husband and wife become competitors. Let me explain.

When a conflict of feeling arises in a marriage, what often happens is that husband and wife enter headlong into a power struggle. Each party turns on the full force of his will and the stronger willed of the two prevails. That person prevails not because he or she is right or wiser or more knowledgeable but often because of a brute "strength" which is stronger than a weak opponent. Such "strength" is akin to the unconquerable stubborness of a very spoiled child.

A Christ-centered marriage takes the competition out of marriage because, rather than husband and wife slugging it out, they both submit to Christ's authority over their lives. There is no need to find out which is the stronger willed. Such knowledge is foolish to them. Their question is now: What would our Lord have us both do?

Now the search begins for Christ's answer rather than John's answer or Mary's answer. Sometimes it is a very difficult and time-consuming search because our Lord's will is not always quickly known. Neither am I saying that husband and wife will always "read" Christ the same way. They may come out of their prayer closets with different answers.

At this point there is great danger, again, that the marriage will become competitive. Having avoided the contest of John's will vs. Marys will, they may now enter a horrible crusade in which Christ's will for John is pitted against Christ's will for Mary.

Please understand that I am talking here only about occasional disagreements in a Christian home. Most differences yield to a solution when both parties submit to the lordship of Christ in their lives. Yet there can be honest differences of opinion as to the will of Christ; or it may be that the degree of commitment to Christ differs between husband and wife. What can be done to reach unanimity in this divided marriage? Consider these four suggestions.

(1) Let each position be fully expressed with the full force of appropriate feelings behind them and let matters lie in that state for a time. The purpose of this is not merely to "let those feelings out" (which is of some immediate though superficial value) but to influence and affect each other. It is important that there be no haste in settling the problem. A solution may take some time, so if at all possible steer away

from the false security of a quick decision just for the sake of escaping marital tension. This kind of tension is normal and potentially useful, so make peace with it if you cannot enjoy it.

I know of an instance where this approach was used. A husband had an opportunity to work in Florida. His wife had deep roots in New Jersey. There was real conflict between them. Each expressed himself fully but there was no agreement, only struggle and deep, painful division.

(2) A heroic attempt must be made to compromise, as it was in this case. Each party needed to give up something of what he was demanding. That, it seems to me, is as it should be in a compromise. In this particular case, it took the form of a number of concessions which the husband gave his wife. He agreed to defer the move to Florida for two years inasmuch as this was agreeable to his company. In order to continue close social ties with people in New Jersey, they agreed that she would spend a week or two visiting each summer. And finally, she even got her husband to agree to using some of their additional income to take some courses at the University of Florida.

There is nothing wrong with this kind of "deal." Indeed, I feel it indicates marital health. This is better than a marriage in which the wife is a sold-out person who has lost all ability to assert her feelings and convictions. A compromise is also better than a marriage in which the husband functions like an army general who has no regard for the feelings of his family. And it is *far* superior to a vicious marital war in which each party is rigid and unbending.

But what if even compromise does not work. Is there anything else that a couple can do? Yes.

(3) They can seek counsel from a third party. Again I recommend your pastor. It is because he is under the same lordship of Christ to which you are committed. Your pastor is trained to know what the Scriptures teach for our lives. True, he is not infallible but he will be indefatigable in his search with you for the meaning of Christ's will for your marriage.

It is a tragedy that many parishioners feel that their pastor is too busy for such work, or would possibly be too greatly shocked by the news of marital tension in their home, or just does not care. Let me speak only for myself. I would far sooner deal with your marital discord than the administrivia which takes up so many hours of my day. In addition, nothing you tell me will shock me, and, be assured, I care.

And what, now, if even counsel does not work?

(4) "Wives, be subject to your husbands, as is fitting in the Lord" (Colossians 3:18). Submit. By so doing you will not only be doing the will of Christ but you will solidly establish your husband as head of your home. No woman should presume to be both head and helpmeet of the same household. It is too much work for one person. God never intended that wives should be so burdened.

Remember, too, that the Scriptures do not say "sell out." They say, "submit." There is a difference. Submission gives you the right to retain your feelings. Keep them. Our Lord does not mean for you to falsify them or abandon them. But submit, nonetheless, and do it not for the sake of your husband or children but for the sake of Christ who asks that you do this. You are not asked to change your mind or feel differently. Christian wives are asked to submit. It is your distinctive spiritual discipline. Your husband has his – ultimate responsibility to Christ for the decision he makes.

Here we conclude our discussion of Christian marriage, having used concrete examples of the operation of people who are in search of a Christian identity.

Let us now turn to the matter of raising children in a Christian home.

Part VI
Leading Children
to a Christian Identity

Chapter Twenty-Eight
The Use of Authority
in the Home

I AM RELUCTANT to add to the tons of advice on raising children which authors have mercilessly thrown at parents, but I choose to add to the literature because something happened in the home of a minister-friend of mine which is so uniquely instructive that it deserves your attention.

This friend has a daughter who is 13 years old. Some time ago she asked her father if she might see a popular horror movie. On the basis of what knowledge he possessed concerning the film, he refused her request even though the child was quite mature for her age. We could argue, perhaps, about whether the child would be damaged by the experience, but my own opinion is that it would be harmful to the girl. I surely wish to support my colleague in his position on this matter. If you wish to read about the spiritual and psychological damage this emotional dynamite does to a child, you might wish to read *Psychotherapy and Religion*[1] by Henry Guntrip.

[1] New York: Harper and Row, 1957.

A week after the girl was denied the right to see the movie, she was invited to a party at a neighborhood friend's. In the course of this party, some of the young people decided to go see a movie and — wouldn't you know it — they chose the forbidden horror film.

Our young friend was in a difficult spot. She was under strong group pressure to go along with her friends whom she definitely did not wish to lose. On the other hand, if she went with her friends, she would be violating the expressed wishes of her parents. What would you have done in such a situation?

Let us pause for a moment to appreciate the fact that this girl, though she is quite young, must be given the freedom to make a decision, even the wrong decision. It seems to me to be inappropriate to say that the girl has no right to choose and must simply obey the command of her father. Don't forget that a 13-year-old lady should be moving in the direction of some self-direction and developing some values and attitudes which are truly her own. So I would wish to give the girl the right to choose either course — but with this freedom, the responsibility to bear the consequences of her decision.

As it turned out, our young friend chose to go to the movie. When she arrived home she was in great distress, however, and she immediately told her mother about her conflict and what she had actually done. If you were the parents of this girl, what would you have done?

Let me tell you how this father handled the problem. He decided, first of all, that the child had violated his expressed decision and that this should entail a penalty. For some time he toyed with the idea of merely excusing the girl's behavior as an act of forgiveness but finally decided against it because it would encourage the child to feel that laws can be broken with impunity. He purposely meant to teach her by his decision that "you get what you pay for" — surely an important piece of reality for us to accept if we wish to become mature. The fact, however, that the girl was young, that she was under tremendous social pressure and that she immediately confided in her mother indicated to the father that the penalty for the disobedience should be tempered with mercy.

You may be interested in the final issue of this episode. The father cut his daughter's allowance for one week as a penalty. On hearing the decision, the girl reacted with anger momentarily but this was followed by expressions of warmth on the part of both father and daughter. The matter was worked through and ended at this point because the authority of the parents was maintained — and every child, particularly adolescents, continually test to see whether the feet of their parents are made of clay or solid metal — and the guilt of the child was eradicated by a sensible punishment.

Have you ever noticed how a small child who has done something wrong, will feel cleansed and forgiven after a well-deserved spanking has been administered? And conversely, how such a child may suffer under a burden of guilt for days if he is ignored?

In this chapter we are talking about parental authority. The example cited is an illustration of where, it seems to me, it is rightfully used. There is a commendable balance of law and grace in this example. It reminds us of the pattern of the Incarnation in which our Lord had to bear the penalty of sin but was sustained and glorified through it. We are reminded that God's dealings with us make use of a proper kind of authority. God is neither authoritarian nor overly permissive. We parents tend at times to be too dictatorial, or, going to the other extreme, to withdraw from the necessary use of authority. Our Lord Jesus Christ by His teachings and deeds has shown us a proper use of an authority which respects both law and grace.

Chapter Twenty-Nine
Give Your Child
Some Disadvantages

PEOPLE SUCH AS you and I sometimes do the rarest things, and here is one which you and I should talk over. I have heard of a married couple with a eight-year-old son who have moved into a university city so that their son can some day study medicine there! But that's not all. It is the fond hope of the parents that this son will practice medicine in the same city in which the parents reside!

I pity both this boy and his mixed-up parents!

Anything and *everything* for the children of today — that seems to be our motto. I remember attending a PTA meeting in which the parents were all trying to think of ways to do more for their children. Someone made a motion that we find part-time jobs for the children. The idea appealed to most everyone except a lonely dissenter who suggested that the kids go out and find their own jobs. He and I were the only votes against the motion.

I see parents knocking themselves out to chauffeur their children anywhere. When these children become teen-agers, they are often given a car and a credit-card to go where they please, when they please. One such child, now 25 years old, has burned out two cars already, and has the added distinction of never having paid a cent of room and board money to his needy parents. When I suggested to the parents that they "boot him out" the parents were horrified.

At the risk of losing even more reputation, I offer this advice: GIVE YOUR CHILD SOME DISADVANTAGES. Really. Children *need* some.

Let us hear Stella Chess in her *Introduction to Child Psychiatry:*[1]

> The child who is never frustrated, whose conflicts are resolved for him by eliminating or easing those factors which militate against the spontaneous expression and satisfaction of his desires, becomes well adjusted only to an extremely artificial set of circumstances. When such a youngster approaches those later stages of socialization which his parents do not control, as on reaching school age, he will lack the kind of experience that would help him know how to respond to each new situation.

What this means is that over-protection and over-concern lead to the under-development of the child. The parent who is always rushing in with "help," always straightening out the road, always rescuing the child – that parent is really damaging the child. The child needs something to challenge him; else he will not grow. The child needs to make mistakes to learn what not to do. When Johnny exchanges his new wagon for a broken sling-shot, he should not be rescued (but neither should he be denounced). It is best if his parents simply accept Johnny with his bad

[1] New York: Grune and Stratton, Inc., 1959, p. 28. Used by permission.

deal and encourage him to earn some money for a new wagon. This encourages Johnny to face his problem and work himself out of it rather than avoid it.

The day is past when we can think of our children as passive little creatures whose proper development can be insured only by providing them with an ideal environment in which to grow. The fact is, that children, even babies, are not passive little creatures but dynamic persons who are continually making choices. Nor is their environment always ideal. Babyhood and childhood are some of the most difficult days of our years. Yet God wisely intended that out of the interaction between the choosing person and his challenging environment, human growth should take place.

To be sure, a child may confront obstacles and problems too great for him to handle, and if he is not assisted and supported by older people, he may be damaged. Psychiatrists have done well in alerting the public to the dangers of the "traumatic episode." But the point I make here is that there is a difference between a crisis and a trauma. When the parents of a small child wish to go out for an evening, and leave the child in the hands of a good baby-sitter with assurances that they will soon return, a crisis may result — but hardly a trauma which will damage the child for many years.

Let children go through their little crises. It is the training period for the greater crises to follow.

Chapter Thirty
Attitudes Toward Mothers

ONE OF THE THINGS I like so much about being a Christian is that in the words and deeds of our Lord, we have a clear picture of interpersonal health. Take, for example, in this matter of selecting the appropriate attitudes toward our mothers—Jesus has shown us the way. We value the help and opinions of teachers, psychiatrists, sociologists, parents, and anyone else who has studied children—but the Way, the Truth and the Life has already been revealed. I would like to sketch the pattern of our Lord's attitudes toward His mother, noting particularly how appropriate was His attitude in each stage of his development.

Jesus began His earthly life with an attitude (if we may speak of a baby having an attitude) of complete dependence upon His mother. This was both necessary and fitting because He was a helpless baby.

The next glimpse we see of Jesus is after He had passed through the dependence of childhood and had become an adolescent. We see Him in His twelfth year talking to some astonished rabbis in the synagogue. Adolescence is a time of breaking free from our dependence upon parents. It is a time of revolt, of becoming an individual. Adolescents are *supposed* to do that. It is appropriate, even though it throws the parents into confusion. And did not Jesus do just that? He abandoned His parents, sat down with the rabbis and freely gave answers to their questions and then had the audacity to say to His complaining mother, "How is it that you sought me? Did you not know that I must be in my Father's house?"

Talk about adolescent revolt! Look here, all teen-age people, how Christ sanctifies your rebellion! But perhaps you should take even greater notice of these words: Jesus "was obedient to [His parents]...and Jesus increased in wisdom and stature, and in favor with God and man" (Luke 2:49,51,52).

At the age of 30, we find that our Lord gently informs His mother that He will not be coerced by her. She calls to Him for wine at the wedding feast and her request is denied until she concedes His complete freedom to act in accordance with His own judgment. The day of obedience to Mary is past. He owes her honor, but not obedience.

The next stage of development was our Lord's "transfer" to another family — the spiritual family of those who believed in Him. The biological family is replaced by a large community of believers. This is the meaning of that episode when Mary and the brothers of Jesus try to gain entrance to the home where He was preaching. They suspected that Jesus was becoming psychotic. When Jesus heard of their efforts He asked, "Who are my mother and my brothers?" Then looking at His audience He said, "Here are my mother and my brothers! Whoever does the will of

God is my brother, and sister, and mother" (Mark 3:31-34). That statement hurt Mary no doubt, but the words had to be said to a mother who was still attempting to protect and mother her 30-year-old son.

The last glimpse of our Lord's dealings with His mother is at the cross (John 19:25-27). When Jesus looked upon her sorrow, He responded with a most appropriate kind of love. There are many kinds of love but one of its best expressions and surely the most timely with an aging mother is the love which *cares—caring* in the sense of doing what is good for another. Jesus commits her to the care of John. The aging Mary is becoming a dependent person once again. She needs someone upon whom she can lean. What the Savior cannot Himself do, He requests of the "disciple whom he loved." As the baby Jesus was dependent upon Mary, so is Mary now returned to dependence upon her surrogate-son John.

I am struck at this point with the amount of pain endured by Mary and Jesus in their relationship. Why was it so painful? The reason is not hard to understand. A mother and her child almost invariably sense themselves to be a part of each other, like an extension of their beings. Each finds it very difficult to say, "I am I and you are you." On the other hand there is a powerful urge to be separate, to have different identities, for every mother has a deep longing to be independent from the child just as the child wants freedom from the mother. It is the clashing of these two basic feelings both within and outwardly between the mother and child that causes us such pain. Jesus did not seek to avoid this pain because He understood it was built into the human situation, but

He was always sensitive to it and understanding of it. He gave both Mary and Himself the right to suffer in this experience.

This is the Way. It is the way to maturity and the development of one's own values. This is the Truth.

Our Lord encourages us to be individuals—people who, when we have grown up, choose to honor but not necessarily obey our parents for "we must obey God rather than men" (Acts 5:29). This is the Life.

Chapter Thirty-One
The Oppression
of Adults by Children

"...babes shall rule over them...the youth will be insolent to the elder...My people—children are their oppressors.
Isaiah 3:4,5,12

THERE ARE MANY parents today who are dedicated more to their children than to God. As I talk to parents with children, I hear some of them saying things like this:

"The only reason I am working 14 hours a day is for my kids. I want them to have the advantages I didn't have."

"I don't care what happens to me but I want my children to have it easier than I had it. I could not go to college. I had to work, you know. But I want my children to go through college."

"My wife and I would get a divorce if it were not for the children.* I can't see breaking up their home."

*I certainly do not recommend a divorce in such a case. This is the time for the parents to seek counsel and begin to grow up, for I have never yet seen two really incompatible people in marriage.

"My children mean more to me than anything else in the world."

It is possible for parents to make gods of their children and then offer themselves as human sacrifices to these children. In the ancient days the parents sacrificed their children. Today we see the opposite—we allow the children to sacrifice the adults.

I have some good historical evidence for that. More than once, history has been steered by the tyranny of children and teen-agers—the Children's Crusades, the Flagelantes, the St. Vitus' Dance. But perhaps the classic example is to be found in the witch-trials in Salem, Massachusetts around 1692.

The Puritans had barely established themselves in the New World when a group of a dozen or so hysterical girls (and one boy) began to make indiscriminate accusations against the most godly people in Salem. Marion L. Starkey in *The Devil in Massachusetts*[1] tells how an undisciplined teen-ager, for example, would accuse a woman of being a witch because the young girl had seen the accused in a spectral vision. This was all that was necessary for the authorities to arrest the accused and take her into court. The spectral evidence was then presented and concurrently with it the teen-agers would usually go into a hysterical trance right there in the first pew of the meeting house. No more convincing proof could be given the judges and forthwith, the witch was condemned to die. As Miss Starkey says: "The idle words of a pack of undisciplined girls were allowed to out-

[1] Gloucester, Mass.: Peter Smith, Publisher. (Also in a Doubleday Dolphin edition.)

weigh whole lifetimes of decency and good faith" (p. 259).

I know of some churches, particularly some small churches, where that same sort of thing goes on today. Understand me, I do not mean witch-trials. But in some churches the power-people are the children. The tyranny of children is a sociological fact in certain congregations and most amazing, the children are enthroned as tyrannical rulers by the adults! Whenever the ultimate concern of a congregation is for their youth, we have a situation in which the church is really ruled by children, for their needs dictate what the church does.

Our youth are thus often given highest priority in the congregation. In them rests the hopes of the adults for the future of the church. For the welfare of the youth, the congregation will often extend a call to a young minister who, if he accepts, is expected to hold on to the young people by means of an active youth program. Sermons must be simple enough to have appeal to young people. We provide a program of activities for the season and a superb taxi service made up of the car-owners in the congregation. No other age group gets such treatment.

Please understand that I am not opposed to youth, nor to the programs we offer them. What I oppose is the idolatry of children and the sacrifice of adults on that pagan altar. This is bad for adults and bad for children. Let us take a look at the damage it does.

Whenever a parent "lives for his children" we know that such a parent is living what Dr. Paul Tournier calls a "provisional existence." Such a person never really lives in reality as an authentic human being. He shifts between living in his own past and his child's future. It is seldom that he enters the present moment in which he, as a person, is a reality. When this becomes a way of life, he feels like a phantom rather than a somebody.

In addition to this problem, our provisional man becomes preoccupied with the world of things. When other people try to enter his cold world of things, he transforms them into "things" by using them as means to his ends. It is not strange that in such a depersonalized world, he never confronts himself as a person. He deeply believes in the denial of himself as a person. He lives for others – in this case, his children – without attempting to live himself. It is a most subtle and satanic kind of suicide in operation here.

What effect does this have on children? They become the bearers of a power over adults which they were never intended to possess. This whole arrangement swells their pride and vanity. Where do they get this power? It is projected into them by defaulting adults who insist on living provisionally. In addition, such a situation teaches the child to repeat the process when he is biologically able to produce his own children.

What, then, might be a Christian view of the child? Ideally, we should live in a Christ-oriented adult world into which children in due time may and do come. It is contrary to God's intention that our adult years be used only to expend ourselves on the younger generation. The attention of adults, it would seem, should be focused on productivity in the kingdom of God, on savoring the deeply satisfying blessings of our mature years and on cherishing the costly wisdom which God bestows on those who have borne their crosses with patience and faith.

I am frank to say that I would not trade places with any person younger than I. The adult years are far more satisfying than the formative years. Many older people have told me that the worst years of their lives were the high-school years. I agree, and find it difficult to understand why any adult would elude the blessings of the latter years by this fascination with childhood and adolescence.

Above all, God intends for our children to eventually mature into the stature of the fullness of Christ. They can do this only if their parents have already attained some of that maturity. This maturity has as its first principle that we are to be subject unto no power but Christ and live unto no goal but His glory. This will then necessarily exclude children as the ultimate sources of power and as the primary goals of our lives.

Conclusion

Conclusion

THE PURPOSE of this book is not new or original. It is simply to help form in us the mind of Christ, to assist us in following in His footsteps, to stamp us with an identity which is authentically Christian—each of these phrases says essentially the same thing. Each chapter was selected to contribute to this goal. Some basic problems in human life were redefined and reshaped in the hope that the "set" of problems God has currently given us may yield to better solutions.

I believe that the major issues of human life today are the same as those with which our early ancestors struggled and with which our children after us will struggle. We have asked and always will ask, "What is my identity? How can I become a whole person before God and with people? Where is the victory over sin? How can I mature as a person and effectively play the roles (such as being a husband or a parent) to which God has called me?" We struggled with each of these questions.

And the answer, in a word, is not a set of ideas but a person—Christ.

I remember during my early years at college that I despised that answer. It was too simple for my psuedo-sophisticated mind. I wrote off Christ as the answer by saying that the word was a cliché, a word with no meaning for us modern people. Twentieth-century man, I argued, needed new, more relevant answers to his changing questions about life. I wanted an answer constructed out of ideas (my own, preferably) which would pass the test my own arrogance had set up.

But God had mercy on my ignorance. Someone who is at once a Person, a pattern and a power came into my life. God took me off the throne of my egoistic omniscience and gave me an answer—the Lord Jesus Christ. The answer to human problems is a Person. I do not exclude knowledge and insight, but look first to the Person, Jesus Christ, who waits to form us into His image so that we may possess His identity.

Then we become somebody. Once we were nobodies. "Once you were no people but now you are God's people; once you had not received mercy but now you have received mercy" (I Peter 2:10).

A new identity has been given us. We are God's own people. "You are a chosen race, a royal priesthood, a holy nation, God's own people..." (I Peter 2:9).

We even bear the name of the Son of God. The name *Christian* identifies us. We are Christ's kind of people. We belong to God.

The search for a Christian identity ends in the discovery of that fascinating Person, Jesus Christ.